A CONCISE HISTORY OF PHILADELPHIA

By Ron Avery

4/23/06

To Bonnie

Hope you enjoyed Philadelphia

Ron Avery

OTIS BOOKS
Philadelphia

OTIS BOOKS

Cover and Book Design by Hoffman Studio
Cover Photo by Alejandro Alvarez
Printed by George H. Buchanan Company, Philadelphia
Photos by Alejandro Alvarez, Sam Psoras, Philadelphia Museum of Art,
Independence National Park, City of Philadelphia.
Library of Congress Catalog: 99-075779
All rights reserved. Copyright © 1999 by Ron Avery
Printed in the United States of America
ISBN 0-9658825-1-9

CONTENTS

A CONCISE HISTORY OF PHILADELPHIA

INTRODUCTION

Those quaint brick houses, courtyards and narrow alleys are not a movie set; it's real history. Some 2,000 18th-century buildings and countless thousands dating to the 19th century are all authentic. In Philadelphia, history seems to ooze up from the sidewalks.

There are still clear marks on the walls of an 18th-century mansion left by cannonballs fired during the Battle of Germantown. The wood floor of another Germantown house still bears the blood stains left by a dying British general.

Philadelphia's remarkable past illustrates nearly every major theme of American history: European settlement, Indian displacement, revolution and independence, immigration, class conflict, industrialization, Civil War, big-city politics, suburbanization, urban decline and the saga of African-American history.

Countless popular and scholarly books focus on various aspects of Philadelphia's past, institutions and personalities. Despite so much attention, a void remains. There is no brief book that tells the entire Philadelphia story.

In fact, only one comprehensive city history was written during the entire 20th century. Published in 1982, "Philadelphia A 300-year History" is a superb collaboration by 20 noted scholars. It has been jocularly labelled "The 300-Pound History" because of its 800-page length.

We believe this book fills the needs of tourists, students, newcomers and Old Philadelphians seeking a readable account of Philadelphia's past in a concise, easy-to-digest package.

"A Concise History of Philadelphia" examines all the major themes and important events in the Delaware Valley from the first 17th-century settlers to the brink of a new millennium.

The challenge was to tell the full story while keeping it concise and interesting. Certainly, some events and personalities are missing from these pages. On the other hand, we couldn't resist the urge to spice the narrative with colorful anecdotes. The fate of General William Howe's lost dog and the breakfast menu of gluttonous Senator Boies Penrose are historically unimportant. But such tidbits humanize history and often linger in the memory after more weighty matters become hazy.

The book is organized chronologically except for the last chapter, which examines the black experience in Philadelphia. Addressing African-American history over the entire 300-year period provides revealing insights into the black condition today.

Thumbnail sketches of some notable Philadelphians who are not included in the main text are provided as an appendix. Finally, the book provides a list of suggested reading; books for the layman that are skillfully and colorfully written.

We hope this concise history will stimulate the reader to learn more, visit more historic sites and care more passionately about preserving a matchless historical heritage.

LENAPE, DUTCH, SWEDES AND FINNS

Before bringing on William Penn and his Quakers, a motley crew of characters must be briefly trotted out on stage. The players include Henry Hudson, an Englishman working for the Dutch; Peter Minuit, a Dutchman working for the Swedes; exiled convicts; a lesbian queen; a 400-pound governor of New Sweden dubbed "The Tub" and peg-legged Peter Stuyvesant.

We invoke Hudson because he was the first European briefly to probe and describe Delaware Bay during his 1609 explorations on the ship Half Moon. He concluded that it was not a northwest passage to Asia and named his find the South River (Zuydt in Dutch). His discovery of the North River (the Hudson) seemed more promising. Hudson's initial exploration allowed the Dutch to claim the Hudson and the Delaware valleys as part of its New Netherland colony.

In 1610, only a year after Hudson's arrival, a second European discovered the same bay and gave it a new name. Sir Samuel Argall was blown off course sailing from the starving colony of Jamestown, Virginia, to Bermuda to fetch food. He ended up off Cape Cod. On his return trip, Argall came upon the same bay and named it to honor his boss, Virginia Governor Thomas West. Governor West also held a title: 12th Lord De la Warr – a place name contracted into "Delaware." Thus the man whose title is affixed to a great river, a state, and even an Indian tribe, never saw the Delaware River.

In the next few years the Dutch did some exploring and name giving. Captain Cornelius Mey provides the name Cape May; Cornelius

Henderickson sailed up the South River and found the mouth of a tributary that was obscured by vegetation. He named it the Hidden River, "Schuylkill" in Dutch.

The Dutch tried to exploit their American lands through a business venture chartered in 1621, The Dutch West India Company. Most of the company's efforts were concentrated along the Hudson, with headquarters on the island of Manhattan. Dutch traders began visiting the Delaware, and in 1623 the company built a log trading post called Fort Nassau at present-day Gloucester, N.J. It wasn't much of a fort and was manned only during times when Indian trading parties arrived. About the same time, the Dutch planted three or four families of Belgian Walloons on what appears to be Burlington Island near present-day Burlington, N.J. Unprotected and unsupported, they abandoned the site after one year and returned to Manhattan. Fort Nassau stood for 28 years before it was abandoned as worthless to Dutch defense and a poor location to trade with Indians traveling from the interior of Pennsylvania.

The first halfhearted Dutch attempt to settle the Delaware was followed by a disastrous settlement in 1631 at Lewes called Swanendael (Valley of the Swans.) Its history is reminiscent of the lost colony of Roanoke, Va., but a bit less mysterious. Individual investors from the Dutch West India Company landed 28 Dutchmen on the bay at Lewes Creek. They built a stockade and a barracks and cleared fields with the aim of planting tobacco and catching whales in the bay. They attempted to befriend the local Indians but a dispute over a trivial matter led to disaster.

During a ceremony that included the firing of a gun salute, the Dutch placed a stake in the ground containing a tin medallion bearing the seal of the States General of the United Netherlands. One Indian pried off the plate with the intention of making a smoking pipe. The Dutch were incensed by this affront.

What happened next is not entirely clear. According to an account provided by the Indians, they executed the culprit to appease the Dutch, but the dead man's family and supporters took revenge and massacred the entire settlement.

When David De Vries, a financial backer of the settlement, visited the site some months later he found "the ground bestrewed with the heads and bones of the murdered men." All the settlers had been killed, their cattle and dogs butchered. De Vries coaxed the story of the stolen medallion from some reluctant Indians.

Seven years passed without further attempts at European settlement. Then in 1638 a new chapter opened with the creation of "New Sweden" on land that was clearly part of New Netherland.

Swedish King Gustavus Adolphus, a great military mind, had planned to get into the business of building colonies for trade in the New World but died in battle before he could realize those aims. His six-year-old daughter, Christina, was to inherit the throne, but until she reached age 18 a group of noblemen ran the country, with Count Axel Oxenstierna at its head.

With the financial backing and expertise of several disgruntled ex-officials of the Dutch West India Company, Oxenstierna formed a similar corporation, the New Sweden Company. One of those Dutchmen (actually a French Huguenot) was Peter Minuit, the first director general of the Dutch West India Company — the same man who made the legendary $24 deal with the Indians for Manhattan. He was also the man who set up Fort Nassau on the Delaware. Here was someone who knew the Indians, the fur trade and the lay of the land — the unpopulated, unlucky land along the Delaware River.

With Minuit in command, the new venture fitted out two ships, the Kalmar Nyckel and the Grip, and with an estimated 60 or 70 men arrived on the Delaware in March 1638. Minuit tried not to make the Swedish presence known to the Dutch, who were in the peak of the trading season at Fort Nassau. He sailed out of view into the Christina River to a rocky ledge in present-day Wilmington. There the Swedes built a stockade called "Fort Christina" in honor of the now 12-year-old future queen and started buying land from the local Indians. The Dutch soon learned of the Swedes and registered a protest. Minuit ignored the threats because his small contingent outnumbered the tiny Dutch detachment.

As a footnote, the ship Grip sailed to the Caribbean for supplies and returned with an African-born slave named Anthony. So, the first black in the Delaware Valley was here 44 years prior to William Penn's founding of Philadelphia. Anthony remained at Fort Christina for at least nine years, according to records.

Minuit left for Sweden aboard the Kalmar Nyckel to report on his progress. Enroute, the ship made a stop at a small Caribbean Island where Minuit visited a Dutch ship anchored in the harbor. A sudden hurricane sank that ship, killing Minuit, but the Kalmar Nyckel escaped serious damage.

Despite a few sizable cargoes of fur, New Sweden was a financial bust. It failed just as miserably in attracting settlers. There were no good reasons for any Swede to pick up stakes and move to a dangerous wilderness. Few immigrants could be enticed voluntarily, so petty criminals, army deserters, vagrants and debtors were forcibly deported. Many were Finns because Finland was then under Swedish control, and the Swedes tended to treat them as troublemakers.

There was only sporadic contact with Sweden, and the tiny population of the colony never numbered more than 500 men, women and children. In 1643 a new governor arrived at the Swedish outpost. Johan Printz was a military man who weighed about 400 pounds; he was dubbed "the Tub" by settlers and "Big Belly" by the Indians. The new governor was headstrong and arrogant and mostly disliked by the settlers, who soon filed petitions complaining of his management style. Some settlers and soldiers returned to Sweden, and a few even ran off to Maryland. Printz counted 183 residents total in New Sweden in 1647. His contract with the company was for a three-year period. But no replacement was sent, and four years passed without mail from his superiors. After nine years on the job, Printz took matters into his own hands by leaving for New Amsterdam and booking passage home, leaving his son-in-law in charge.

Printz did try to improve and expand the tiny colony. He had a flour mill built on Cobbs Creek. He rebuilt Fort Christina and created new forts and blockhouses. Fort Elfsborg, erected on the New Jersey shore, was eventually abandoned under the relentless attack of Jersey mosquitoes that bred in the surrounding swamps and tormented the soldiers day and night.

A fort called New Gothenburg was built in conjunction with a two-story house with brick fireplace for Printz, his wife and five daughters at a place referred to as Tinicum Island. The spot was below the present Philadelphia Airport and was not a real island but a piece of ground on the river with a creek behind it.

New Sweden was not a happy place. Printz hanged one settler accused of plotting a mutiny. Many died of illness, and "peaceful" Lenape Indians were not practicing pacifism. In one letter Printz writes, "Our savages have become very proud here. . . . they murdered a man and a woman in their beds, and they killed a few days afterward two soldiers and a servant." Printz longed for "a couple of hundred soldiers . . . then with the help of God not a single savage would be allowed to live on the river."

Printz's successor, Johan Rising, had similar complaints: "Our neighbors the Renappi (Lenape) threaten not only to kill our people in the land and ruin them before we can become stronger and prevent such things, but also to destroy the trade (with other tribes). . . . We must daily buy their friendship with presents for they are and continue to be hostile and worse than they have been hitherto. . . . Last winter one of them killed a woman not far from here."

While dealing with the Lenape could be deadly for the Swedes, their "wars" with the Dutch for control of the region were bloodless charades. The Dutch were certainly upset by the Swedish forts and the competition for Indian trade. But the two nations were at peace, and neither wanted to risk real war over such a remote and relatively unimportant outpost.

Still, Printz and his counterpart in New Amsterdam, Peter Stuyvesant, were both proud military men, and it was inevitable that they would butt heads. The Dutch kicked it off by building a blockhouse on the Schuylkill River called Fort Beversreede to intercept Indian trading parties arriving from the interior of Pennsylvania. The Swedes attempted to tear it down and built their own post nearby, blocking access to the river. In 1651 Stuyvesant collected 120 soldiers and marched overland to Fort Nassau on the Delaware. At the same time 11 Dutch ships sailed up the Delaware. It was a tremendous show of power for such a sparsely populated area. Printz was badly outnumbered and outgunned and offered no resistance. Stuyvesant then built a major fortress, Fort Casimir, and established a Dutch town next to it called New Amstel, which the English would rename New Castle.

In 1654, Printz's replacement, Rising, arrived with a contingent of 200 new settlers. The Dutch were asleep at Fort Casimir with only nine soldiers in the fort and no gunpowder for their cannons. Rising politely requested the commander to surrender. Fort Casimir changed hands without a shot being fired. Rising magnanimously invited the Dutch settlers to stay.

This was too much for Stuyvesant. He returned to the Delaware a year later with a fleet of small ships and about 350 fighting men. This time it was the Swedes' turn to surrender without firing a shot. But the irascible Stuyvesant had chosen a terrible time for his assault on the Delaware. While the governor and his troops were away, an Indian raiding party of 500 braves attacked New Amsterdam and was repulsed with great losses.

The Dutch attack on the Delaware was the official end to New Sweden, after only 17 years. Yet, Stuyvesant couldn't have been nicer. Swedes who wanted to return home could sail at Dutch expense. Those electing to stay on the Delaware could keep their property and enjoy full citizenship and freedom of worship. Only 35 decided to leave.

Swedish interest in the area waned with the ascent of oddball Queen Christina. The queen – who tried her best to be crowned king – spent money lavishly, refused to marry and voluntarily abdicated the throne. She dressed as a man, had several affairs with women, moved to Rome, converted to Catholicism and later tried unsuccessfully to get her crown back.

New Netherland would not last long. In 1664 the English decided it was time to consolidate their colonial empire in North America. It had always made claims to the region based on the alleged prior discovery of John Cabot. An overwhelming British naval force sailed to New York. The feisty Stuyvesant wanted to fight, but the frightened burgers of New Amsterdam insisted on surrender.

The European impact on the Lenape Indians of the Delaware Valley was to prove near fatal. The white man offered fabulous trading goods. Imagine what it was like to obtain metal knives and hoes, iron pots and kettles, firearms and cloth for people whose tools were all stone and bone, whose pots were clay, who hunted with arrows and wore only furs.

For these European treasures, they traded beaver and other animal skins and sold the same land to the Dutch, Swedes and English with little concept of what they were losing. Native Americans felt they could no more sell the land than they could sell the air. They naively believed they were sharing the land, not abandoning it forever.

The tribe was decimated by European diseases including smallpox and measles. One writer estimates the Lenape dwindled from about 24,000 in 1630 to 3,000 by the year 1700.

Like other East Coast tribes, the Lenape were pushed ever farther westward. They settled in Ohio, were uprooted to Indiana, then were pushed to Missouri and Kansas. After the Civil War the major remnant of the tribe was moved onto a Cherokee reservation in Oklahoma. Lenape live today in Canada and Oklahoma, but practically no one can speak the native tongue.

WILLIAM PENN:
17TH-CENTURY FLOWER CHILD

Unlike Benjamin Franklin, few modern folks have a sharp image of William Penn. But it's easy to get a handle on the youthful Penn for those with memories of 1960s "flower children," hippie non-conformists who rejected "the establishment" and embraced exotic cults.

Here was a rich kid who defied parental authority, rejected the values and ways of society and linked his fate to an outcast religious cult. Penn was expelled from college, estranged from his father and jailed for his nonconformist, obstreperous ways. Here was a 17th-century flower child who talked and wrote endlessly of "peace and love."

To understand William Penn it is first necessary to know something of his father, whose name was also William: Admiral Sir William Penn. The name "Pennsylvania" honors Sir William, not his son. The Admiral fought for Cromwell and Parliament in the English Civil War that saw the beheading of King Charles I in 1649. Conversely, the Admiral was apparently one of those who plotted the restoration of the Stuart monarchy and was briefly jailed.

When Parliament returned Charles II to the throne, the Admiral was sent to Holland to escort the new King home. Even before the ship reached land, the Admiral was knighted. Obviously, the Stuarts owed a debt of gratitude to Admiral Penn.

The Admiral's wealth was based on rents for lands he owned in England and Ireland. His first and only surviving son, William, was born in London in 1644. Historians described the youngster as serious, introspective, bookish. At 17, he was enrolled at Oxford University and claimed he was "banished" in his second year. The expulsion had nothing to do with student high jinks or misdeeds. On the contrary, young William was too serious. He saw Oxford as a "place of idleness, loose living, profaneness, prodigality, a den of gross ignorance and debauchery." Somehow his outspoken, high-minded opinions got Penn expelled.

The hot-tempered Admiral was enraged. Young Penn was whipped, tossed out of the house briefly and then sent off to Paris, where the Admiral hoped his son would gain maturity and polish in Europe's most elegant capital. Indeed, serious-minded William returned home displaying foppish mannerisms and a stylish wardrobe.

Penn studied law for awhile, sailed briefly with his father during a war with Holland, took charge of family land in Ireland and there, as a civilian volunteer, helped put down an army mutiny. But it was in Ireland at age 23 that Penn would put aside his sword, join the Religious Society of Friends and find his life's work.

The founder of the sect was George Fox, a charismatic itinerant preacher with little formal education. Fox was a riveting speaker who advocated a return to a "primitive Christianity" without clergy, dogma or churches. The faith's key tenet holds that the Divine Spirit could speak directly to every person. They believe there is a spark of God in all men, creating a highly egalitarian movement.

We should not confuse the first generation of Quakers with the popular image of quiet, introspective, plain folks. On the contrary, they were fanatical firebrands who proclaimed their beliefs in the most dramatic and provocative style – zealots who often courted martyrdom.

Great Britain in the 17th century was bubbling with religious ferment. Of the many offbeat sects, the Friends attracted the most attention and converts from every social class. Government policy toward such nonconforming sects vacillated between bloody persecution – brandings, whippings, hangings, imprisonment – to reluctant toleration. During the Friends' first 40 years (1652 is considered the founding date) an estimated 15,000 Quakers were imprisoned and some 450 died in jail.

The first use of the word "Quaker," according to Fox, came when he stood in front of a magistrate and declared, "Tremble before the Lord." The judge replied, "You are the Quaker, not I."

They alienated and irritated the establishment with their pacifism, refusal to doff their hats to anyone, including royalty or judges, and the use of familiar "thee" and "thou" instead of "you" to their betters. They took Christ's injunction, "Swear not at all" literally, refusing to take an oath in court or even swear an oath to prove they were not Catholics.

Penn had been mightily impressed as a 12-year-old child by the words of Quaker preacher Thomas Loe. Now as a young man, Penn learned Loe was preaching in Cork. He listened and almost immediately joined the sect. He was still wearing his fancy gentlemen's clothes and sword a few weeks later when he was arrested for the first time at a Quaker meeting.

Penn would get to know Britain's most hellish prisons, including the Tower of London and fetid Newgate. He would eventually reconcile with his father and use his family's wealth and position to aid the persecuted faith.

In 1674, Penn married an attractive, blonde Quakeress, Gulielma Springett; they produced six children. She died in 1694, and Penn married Hannah Callowhill, who was 24 years his junior and produced seven more Penn children. Only two children from the first marriage and four from the second lived to full adulthood.

Penn was a prolific writer who churned out 150 books, essays and pamphlets, most on religion. During a seven-month stay in the Tower of London he sketched out his major opus, *"No Cross, No Crown."* It urges a return to the virtues and simplicity of early Christianity, exhorting readers to "choose the good paths of temperance, wisdom, gravity and holiness."

"Some Fruits of Solitude" is a collection of simple maxims and proverbs. Ben Franklin polished up many Penn proverbs and placed them in the mouth of Poor Richard. Does Penn's "haste makes work which caution prevents" have a familiar ring?

Penn was a "gentleman," who never held a regular job. He was terrible at money management. But he shouldered responsibilities for Quaker leadership, which included proselytizing trips to Europe, where he met with persecuted religious sects in Germany.

Quakers, including George Fox, considered immigration to North America. Some Quaker zealots went to Massachusetts to rail against the Puritans. They were banished knowing that if they returned they could be whipped, imprisoned and mutilated. At least three who couldn't resist entering the lion's den had their ears chopped off. Enraged Puritans passed a law that made Quaker preaching a capital offense. Four Quakers who took up the challenge were promptly hanged.

Friends settled peacefully in tolerant Rhode Island, and a large Quaker community grew up in North Carolina. In 1674 Quakers Edward Billinge and John Fenwick purchased the colony of West Jersey. (New Jersey was divided into two separate colonies.) Salem and Burlington on the east bank of the Delaware River were growing Quaker towns a half dozen years before Philadelphia was born. When Fenwick and Billinge got into a dispute, Penn served as a Quaker arbitrator. This involvement may have started him thinking about the mostly vacant land on the west bank of the Delaware.

In 1680 Penn petitioned the crown for a colony in America on the Delaware River between the colonies of Maryland and New York. In less than a year, Penn was granted some 45,000 square miles of virgin forest, making him the world's largest private landowner. The cost: a symbolic payment of two beaver skins a year to the crown. Penn was also to turn over to the crown a fifth of all gold and silver that might be found, but no such riches were discovered.

Some believe the huge land grant was payment of a 16,000-pound debt the King owed to the now-deceased Admiral. In fact, Charles II had a large number of debts, and Parliament had simply declared them all invalid. Legally, there was no debt. But in his charter, the King gratefully acknowledges "the memory and merits of his (Penn's) late father in diverse services and particularly to his conduct, courage and discretion. . . . in that signal battle and victory fought against the Dutch fleet (in 1665)."

The charter also expresses the desire to expand the British Empire, promote new trade and "reduce the savage natives, by gentle and just manners, to the love of civil society and the Christian religion."

Penn wanted to name the colony New Wales after hearing that it looked something likes Wales. When this was rejected, he suggested Sylvania (a woodsy place). "And they (the King and his secretary) added Penn to it," he wrote. "And though I much opposed and went to the king to have it struck out and altered, he said it was passed and he would take it upon him." Vanity was a sin to Quakers, and Penn was so fearful that Friends might think he had named the colony for himself that he tried unsuccessfully to bribe officials to change the name in the final charter.

We will examine Penn's plans, promotional activity and governance of his new colony in the next chapter, but let us now sum up the rest of the founder's rather unhappy life.

Penn received his charter from Charles II in 1681 and died in 1718. He spent only four of those 37 years in Pennsylvania, two visits of approximately two years each – 1682-1684 and 1699-1701.

It can be said that the colony provided more grief and anguish than pleasure or profit. Problems galore detained Penn in England. There was a boundary dispute with Maryland, enemies in government, debts, disputes with the colonial Assembly. The litany of woes includes the death of a beloved wife and the grief created by a wild and wayward son, Billy.

Penn was a poor manager and a rather poor judge of character. Philip Ford, his business manager, provides a prime example of both. At some point Penn owed Ford about 4,000 pounds in back pay and cash Ford loaned from his own pocket. Penn gave Ford a mortgage on Pennsylvania as security. Things became more complex when Penn "sold" Pennsylvania to Ford, who leased it back to Penn in a legal fiction that would benefit both men. But when Ford died his will claimed an 11,000-pound debt and title to Pennsylvania that should be sold by his heirs if Penn did not pay within six months. It took years to untangle the mess, including a brush with debtors' prison. Penn's friends had to loan him money to finally settle the debacle for 7,600 pounds and clear up the title of Pennsylvania.

In disgust, Penn tried to sell Pennsylvania back to the Crown. There were several years of dickering over price, but in 1712 an agreement was reached and Penn accepted a downpayment of 1,000 pounds. In the end, the deal fell through due to objections from creditors and Penn's children. Next, Penn suffered a debilitating stroke.

Fortunately his second wife, Hannah, did have a good head for business. During Penn's final years of declining mental and physical health, Hannah made sound business decisions and appointed competent officials to run the colony.

There is no simple way to sum up the man's life and character. Pennsylvania was almost an instant success that grew rapidly and became prosperous. Yet the proprietor failed to prosper. He urged toleration but was constantly involved in contentious feuds. Quakers preached a simple life, but Penn never gave up the lavish lifestyle to which he was born.

Primarily, he was a political and religious thinker. He was a visionary who proposed both a United Nations-type organization for Europe and "a scheme of union" for the colonies to meet and solve mutual problems.

FRIEND PENN PEDDLES HIS PLAN

King Charles II gave William Penn no choice when he designated Pennsylvania as the name for the new colony. But Penn was able to name his capital city without royal interference. He chose Philadelphia. It's Greek and means brotherly love (*philos*, love or friendship and *adelphos*, brother.) Penn didn't coin the name. There were two Philadelphias in ancient times: at present-day Amman, Jordan, and another Philadelphia in today's Turkey.

Penn had very specific plans for his city, although he left it to aides to rush off to America and find the best location. They chose a place called *Coaquannock*, meaning "pine grove." It was just north of *Wiccaco*, where the Swedes had built a blockhouse used for Lutheran church services. (The blockhouse became brick Gloria Dei or Old Swedes Church in 1700, the oldest house of worship in the city.) Penn was scrupulous in paying for lands claimed by prior settlers and just as conscientious in paying the Indians.

Surveyor Thomas Holme laid out the city according to Penn's instructions with wide, straight streets. Penn described a High Street (now Market Street) and a Broad Street that would each be 100 feet wide. These were wider than any London street; today both are still wide enough to accommodate four lanes of traffic with parking on both sides. Most other streets were 50 feet wide. The city was a grid with streets intersecting at right angles. Radiating out from the city's boundaries are certain diagonal roads, such as Germantown Avenue, Ridge Avenue and

Frankford Avenue. They followed old Indian paths and connected the city to outlying communities.

The city was a rectangle about two miles long from the Delaware to the Schuylkill rivers. It was about a mile wide, from Cedar (South Street) to Vine Street. Penn's original city is today's Center City.

Penn was a country squire who wanted to create "a green country town, which would never be burnt, and always be wholesome." The plan called for about four houses on a block, each with its own spacious garden and orchard. The proprietor also created five public squares for open space.

The founder's dream of a pleasant country town was doomed from the beginning. People crowded together along the Delaware River, close to the heart of trade and business. Few lived beyond 6th street until the 19th century. Very quickly the large building lots disappeared as owners subdivided their plots. Crammed courtyards lined with small rental houses connected to city streets by narrow alleys blossomed. In the end, there was no green space between houses. A good example is seen on Front Street, where Penn's plan laid out 43 building lots. In seven years the owners subdivided them into 70 lots; in 20 years there were 102 properties.

Penn's five park-like squares were superfluous in a forested wilderness. They didn't take on the appearance of recreational parks until the middle of the 19th century. Now-leafy Washington Square was a burial ground for the poor. Public hangings were held in Center Square and Logan Square, which also had burials. All were used as trash dumps. A Friends meeting house built at Center Square (now City Hall) was so distant from where people lived that it was not used and was soon torn down.

If many details of Penn's plan were doomed to failure, the city, as a whole, was an instant success. In less than 20 years, it had 2,500 hard-working residents and the ambience of a bustling seaport and market town. After a quarter of a century, Quakers were a minority in the city, although a politically dominant minority.

Penn was one of the world's pioneer real-estate promoters. He wrote eight promotional tracts, printed in several languages, touting Pennsylvania. The first was published before Penn ever laid eyes on his province, and he candidly declared he would "say little in praise. . . of its soil, air and water." The tract does boast that Pennsylvania was "600 miles closer to the sun than England." The tract provided transportation fees to the colony and offered 5,000-acre plots for 100 pounds. Those who could not afford to buy, could rent. The prices seemed high, and Penn was eventually forced to sell smaller plots. But he gave free bonuses to large buyers: building lots in the city and 80-acre plots just outside city boundaries in open "liberty lands." In the first four years, Penn and his agents sold 700,000 acres to 600 buyers for about 9,000 pounds.

You might think the world's largest private landowner would soon be one of its richest men. It never happened. The proprietor was saddled with start-up costs as well as administrative and governmental expenses. While Penn was an imaginative planner and promoter, he was a poor businessman. A 1704 letter to his secretary, James Logan, laments: "O Pennsylvania, what has thou not cost me! Above 30,000 (pounds) more than I ever got from it, two hazardous and most fatiguing voyages, my straits and slavery here (England) and my son's soul, almost."

Another Penn project – a good idea but another business failure – was a stock company called the Free Society of Traders, founded to build industrial and commercial facilities and promote trade. He granted the corporation sizable lands inside the city and several miles upriver in Frankford, where Swedes had already built a gristmill. The corporation did build mills, brick kilns, tanneries, warehouses and piers, but was a financial failure. Its headquarters were on a slight hill near Front and Pine streets, providing the name "Society Hill" to the entire neighborhood.

It is obvious from Penn's writings that the new colony was not merely a real-estate venture or simply a place of refuge for the Quakers. He was an idealist, steeped in the political philosophy of the era. Penn had either read or consulted the great thinkers on the subject of good government. In one letter Penn uses the phrase "holy experiment" in reference to Pennsylvania. Other writings show his intent was to provide the world an example of what Quaker principles and brotherly love could achieve. Although he was pressured into it by the settlers, Penn eventually created a liberal, democratic form of government (by 17th-century standards) that some say laid the foundation of American democracy.

Penn held the title of Proprietor or Governor, making him the chief executive of the province. He drafted a constitution known as the "Frame of Government" that set up an elected Assembly and Council. The governor would preside over the Council, which would initiate all legislation. The larger Assembly could either approve or reject that legislation. This first "Frame" was far from democratic, and Penn modified it several times. By 1701 the Assembly had full legislative powers, and the Council became a sort of cabinet. The governor could veto laws passed by the Assembly, but neither side could impose its will on the other. Penn needed the Assembly, but the two sides were often at odds. The conflict between governor and Assembly under the proprietorship of Penn's heirs was often bitter.

A hundred years later, the leaders of a new nation would come together in Philadelphia to create the U.S. Constitution but go home without enacting a Bill of Rights for the people. Penn did not forget. His Frame included a Charter of Liberties. It granted the right to vote to free males, with a low requirement for property ownership. There could be no taxation without approval of the Assembly. It provided for speedy jury trial by one's peers in open courts. And it contained an unusual guarantee of religious liberty in an era when most nations (and British colonies) had an official state religion. The Charter of Liberties provided that no one would be "molested or prejudiced for their religious persuasion or practice in matters of faith and worship, nor shall they be compelled at any time to frequent or maintain any religious worship, place or ministry whatever."

Another Penn accomplishment was his ability to win the trust and respect of the Indians. He was fascinated and impressed by the Native Americans, learned their language and wrote an essay speculating that the Indians evolved from the Lost Tribes of Israel. Indian leaders liked Penn. They were told that the name "Penn" could mean a writing quill or feather. So, they called him *"Onas,"* meaning quill or feather. Quakers were called "the children of *Onas.*"

The goodwill and fair treatment established by Penn meant that Pennsylvania had no Indian problems for 70 years. Indians often visited the city. Delegations were sometimes housed in the wings of the State

House (Independence Hall.) Fear that they might set fire to the place prompted the Assembly to build two wooden sheds on the State House grounds as Indian dormitories.

After Penn's death in 1718, the three surviving sons from his second marriage, John, Thomas and Richard, became coproprietors of Pennsylvania. All rejected Quakerism, opting for the more fashionable Church of England. They were mostly absentee owners, ruling from England through appointed deputy governors. Many power struggles would occur between the Penn family and the Assembly; Benjamin Franklin would emerge as the Penns' most militant foe.

Penn gave his father, the Admiral, plenty of heartache and headaches with his stubborn embrace of Quakerism, his activism, arrests and jailings. Penn's son from his first marriage, William, called Billy, would provide the aging Penn a bitter cup of his own medicine. Billy was an obnoxious brat who spent extravagantly, ran up debts, rejected Quakerism and married at age 17 against his father's wishes.

Just as the Admiral had sent his wayward son to Europe in hopes that he would settle down, Penn hoped his prodigal son would benefit from a stay in Philadelphia. In less than a year Billy was back in disgrace. He had become a honcho in an unofficial Philadelphia militia and seemed to be the prime troublemaker in a tavern brawl involving militia and members of the town watch. Legal proceedings were initiated against Billy but later dropped. The ingrate ignored his father during Penn's waning years. He apparently deserted his wife and children and died at age 40 in France, in the midst of a court battle to wrest Pennsylvania away from his stepbrothers.

CHAPTER 4

WOLVES, FISH, MUCK AND MYSTICS

In less than 100 years Philadelphia, a latecomer among the colonies, would grow to become the largest, most cosmopolitan city on the continent. But its early days were as rough-and-ready as any wilderness settlement.

The new colony was paying bounties of 10 to 15 shillings for wolves. You had to present the animal's head to get paid. Those who registered as professional wolf hunters were paid 25 shillings a head. The new government was also paying bounties for the heads of crows and blackbirds, considered to be "very destructive of all sorts of corn and grain." On the other hand, to curb shooting accidents, fines were imposed for "killing with a firearm any pigeon, dove, partridges and other fowl in the open streets of the city of Philadelphia."

The Wild West atmosphere was still evident 70 years after the city's founding, when in 1751 the tiny Jewish community complained that "unthinking people" were using the walls and tombstones of its cemetery for target practice. An early ordinance forbade the sale of liquor to the Indians. Another law barred unscrupulous Indian traders from other colonies from doing business in Pennsylvania.

Sure, the new city had wide streets, but they were unpaved, trash- and manure-filled quagmires for more than 50 years. One disgusted mayor noted that the first impression of visitors to the city was always the "deep and miry streets." So many pigs were running free in the city that a law provided that anyone who caught a free-roaming hog could keep half of the meat, with the other half going to the poor. Many kept cows on their property, and some made a living by taking cows to pasture and returning them at night.

Many of the first immigrants lived temporarily in man-made caves dug into the high riverbanks. In England, Penn was enraged to learn that the caves had become permanent dens of vice and "debauchery." Apparently, many were unlicensed grog shops, brothels and gambling dens catering to sailors and city riffraff. One public scandal involved a seemingly respectable, married lady caught fornicating in one of these hellholes.

Young bucks racing their horses through the city streets was a common hazard. In fact, lightly populated Sassafras Street was an unofficial racecourse that eventually took the name Race Street. In 1726 a grand jury declared that racing on Sassafras Street was "very dangerous to life."

Although many of the first houses were made of wood, brickmaking started early. By 1690, four brickmakers were at work. By the mid-1700s, Philadelphia was predominately a brick city.

It may be today's buzzword, but Penn believed in diversity. Quaker founder George Fox and Penn had preached in Holland and Germany. Penn sent promotional leaflets and sales agents to the Continent; in 1683 the first German (actually Dutch-speaking) Quaker families led by the scholarly Francis Daniel Pastorius arrived from Crefeld. They settled outside the city, in what would become the village of Germantown. Eventually thousands of Germans would flood into Pennsylvania. By the 1740s, German-speakers made up nearly half the population of the colony. The first arrivals were mostly persecuted religious sects: Mennonites, Brethren and Schwenkfelders followed by German Lutherans and Catholics.

The most exotic arrivals were 40 German mystics who arrived in 1694 to meditate in the wilderness and look for signs in the sky heralding the Second Coming of Christ. They settled near Germantown along the scenic Wissahickon Creek, where they built a large log tabernacle. Leader Johannes Kelpius was a healer and scholarly mystic who advocated "perpetual inward prayer." After a number of years, the "Hermits of the Wissahickon" drifted away, but Kelpius remained in the Wissahickon woods, where he died in 1708.

A large group of early settlers were Welsh Quakers, who purchased

40,000 acres west of the city. The area became known as the "Welsh Barony," located in today's Lower Merion, Haverford and Radnor townships.

Small numbers of Italian, French and Swiss arrived. Large contingents of Scotch-Irish from Ulster, Irish Catholics and Scot Presbyterians migrated to the colony. There was a labor shortage, and close to half the newcomers were penniless indentured servants who worked off their passage as near-slaves for three or four years.

Philadelphia became America's largest entry point for immigrants during the 18th century. For example, 7,000 German immigrants arrived in the city in 1754 alone. Many were attracted to Pennsylvania because of its religious tolerance and because no colony could match its fertile soil. Eastern Pennsylvania and Delaware can truly be characterized as the "bread basket" of early America. Wheat and flour were major exports of the Delaware Valley. Perhaps, nowhere in the world did a loaf of bread sell so cheaply.

Its rivers and other streams were teeming with fish and fowl. Every spring enormous schools of shad, herring and giant sturgeon (weighing as much as 400 pounds) surged up the Delaware River and its tributaries to spawn. In April 1778 George Washington's lean troops at Valley Forge gorged themselves during the Schuylkill River shad run. "For almost a month the whole camp stank and men's fingers were oily. In addition, barrels had been held in readiness, and hundreds of these were filled with salted shad for future consumption," wrote one soldier.

In the early 19th century a one-day haul of 3,000 catfish was reported by a single Schuylkill River fisherman using nets strung between the rocks. Its rich resources combined with the energy and enterprise of its population would soon make Pennsylvania and its capital, Philadelphia, a very affluent place.

CHAPTER 5

WEALTH AND OPPORTUNITY
AS REVOLUTION LOOMS

B y the 1760s – as the colonies were inching toward revolution – Philadelphia's population and commerce had outstripped all rivals including Boston, New York and Baltimore.

By 1770 the city had some 25,000 residents (including Southwark and Northern Liberties); New York had some 20,000 residents, while Boston's population stood at 15,000.

The wolves and riverbank caves were gone. Major streets were paved with cobblestones, lighted by whale-oil lamps (when the moon was not bright) and patrolled at night by paid watchmen. The port was lined with scores of wharves and warehouses. About 700 ships came and went annually. There were nine busy shipbuilders.

The city had an almshouse for the poor, a sturdy prison, several volunteer fire companies and a bustling three-block-long market. The city boasted the only public hospital and medical school in the colonies. It had two Roman Catholic churches and a Jewish congregation, plus houses of worship for Baptists, Presbyterians, Methodists and German Reform. Its three Anglican churches included handsome Christ Church with its imposing 196-foot-high steeple, the tallest structure in town.

There was by now a well-established aristocracy – a clique of elite families that would retain its leadership and prestige well into the 20th century. A great deal of intermarriage occurred among these families, whose wealth was usually based on shipping, trade or real estate. Most traced their roots to the earliest Quaker immigrant families that, at some point, switched to the Anglican Church. Families that fit the pattern included the names Biddle, Wharton, Cadwalader, Norris, Morris, Rush, Drinker, Wetherill and Fisher.

Mark Twain's wry observation of the late 19th century was just as true of the late 18th century: "In Boston they ask how much does he know. In New York how much is he worth. In Philadelphia, who were his parents."

The elite families aped the lifestyle and tastes of the British upper class. They hunted foxes, bred race horses, attended balls, formed exclusive clubs, and entertained lavishly in elegantly furnished townhouses and country mansions. One hallmark of the 18th century Philadelphia gentry was ownership of a summerhouse or estate in the suburbs. Many of these mansions survive today overlooking the Schuylkill River in Fairmount Park or in Germantown.

Philadelphians of all classes now had the time and inclination for recreation and fun, and those dour, super-pious Quakers were no longer politically strong enough to stop it. In the colony's early days there were laws prohibiting card playing, theaters, dice, lotteries, dueling, drunkenness, scolding, cursing, swearing, smoking on the streets, drinking healths and a 9 p.m. curfew on taverns.

But Quakers, along with everyone else, did drink beer, wine, cider and other spirits, because many believed that water was not healthful. Philadelphia was saturated with taverns. The first building that greeted the eyes of William Penn when his barge landed at Dock Creek in 1682 was the Blue Anchor Tavern, although some say it was still under construction.

By 1767 there were 153 licensed taverns and many illegal operations – a ratio of one tavern for every 173 men, women and children. Taverns filled many needs. In an era without office buildings, the taverns and coffeehouses (which also served liquor) were the places where business was conducted. Colonial newspapers were filled with notices placed by merchants and ship captains informing buyers that they would conduct business at a certain tavern at a certain hour. The major merchants all chipped in to build the London Coffee House in 1754 to create a nice place for business. In 1773 the merchants built an even more luxurious place. The spacious City Tavern on 2nd Street was ideal for making deals during the day and enjoying the best food and drink at night. Every famous patriot, including Washington, Adams and Jefferson, frequented City Tavern. John Adams declared it "the most genteel (tavern) in America." A replica of the famous watering hole now serves ye authentic olde food and drink to tourists.

At the other extreme was a three-block stretch of Race Street lined by so many sleazy dives that it was known as "Helltown." Here the entertainment centered on gambling, fistfights, cockfights and bull baiting (pitting a bull against a pack of dogs.) Dogs were also the attraction at a tavern on Chestnut Street across from the State House. Its "spit dogs" ran in a hollow cylinder attached to a jack that kept the meat turning over the kitchen fire.

In addition to the merchant elite, another social class was rising rapidly. This class consisted of the skilled artisans, tradesmen and mechanics that included silversmiths, furnituremakers, printers, iron masters and stone masons. The master carpenters, who profited from a never-ending construction boom, typified this class. In 1724 the master carpenters formed a guild called the Carpenters Company. In addition to serving as a beneficial society for members and their widows, it set prices and building standards and provided an exchange of ideas on construction and architecture. In 1774 the organization completed Carpenters Hall as its meeting place just in time to play an important role in the coming American Revolution.

Philadelphia's Number One citizen, Benjamin Franklin, was a member of this skilled "leather apron" class and the prototype for the new, self-made American. Franklin was a 17-year-old runaway apprentice from Boston with only two years of formal education when he arrived practically penniless in Philadelphia in 1723.

The talented and ambitious Franklin prospered along with the city. By age 42 he retired from active business, devoting the next 42 years to politics, civic improvements, science, invention and diplomacy. There were hundreds of similar men throughout the British colonies, but Franklin came to symbolize the "New Man" at his best. America's first celebrity demonstrated that no matter how lowborn, in America a man could rise to his full potential through diligence, virtue and ambition.

So, on the eve of the American Revolution, Philadelphia was growing and prosperous. It had a "silk stocking" elite and a large class of skilled artisans. The classes would sometimes cooperate and sometimes clash during the birth pains of a new nation.

CHAPTER 6

TEA TAX, A DECLARATION, A MYTH ABOUT A BELL

Strangely, it was those radical Bostonians and their "Tea Party" that made Philadelphia the epicenter of the American Revolution.

Friction between the Mother Country and the colonies started in 1765 with new tax policies that were violently protested by a people accustomed to self-government and self-taxation. Philadelphians of all classes seemed united in resisting "taxation without representation." Mass protest meetings brought thousands to the State House (Independence Hall) yard. There were boycotts of British goods and threats and violence directed at tax collectors. In London, Benjamin Franklin argued the Americans' case for Pennsylvania and other colonies.

Things were relatively quiet in 1773 until passions were inflamed again by large shipments of tea to the colonies by the British East India Company. Actually, the price of tea – even with tax– would drop. But the tea deliveries were protested as an "illegal monopoly" harmful to American merchants. There was a determination not to allow the tea to land. In New York and Philadelphia ship captains turned back with their cargos. A Philadelphia group calling itself the "Committee for Tarring and Feathering" sent a persuasive message to the captain of the tea ship Polly with this pointed question, "What think you, Captain, of a halter around your neck, 10 gallons of liquid tar decanted on your pate, with the feathers of a dozen wild geese laid over that to enliven your appearance?"

But it was the dramatic dumping of 342 chests of tea into Boston Harbor that enraged King George III, goading him to actions that led to revolution. As punishment, Boston's harbor was closed until the dumped tea was paid for and "peace and obedience to the law" restored. The city was put under military control with troops quartered in private houses.

On May 19th, 1774, Boston silversmith Paul Revere galloped into Philadelphia to seek support for his city's suffering under Britain's "Intolerable Acts." The next day 300 prominent Philadelphians met at City Tavern to consider Boston's appeal. There was plenty of sympathy throughout the colonies and strong feelings that something should be done or others might share Boston's fate.

For the first time, the American colonies met for joint action. Delegates from 12 colonies (Georgia did not attend) arrived in Philadelphia in September 1774 for the First Continental Congress. Philadelphia was chosen because it was large and offered all the comforts. But it was also chosen for its "keystone" location. A keystone is the center stone in an arch. And Pennsylvania was the convenient "keystone" of British North America: six colonies to the north, six to the south.

The delegates met at the new Carpenters Hall. Philadelphia merchant Charles Thomson was named secretary, a role he would ably fill until the end of the Revolutionary War. In 1774 no one wanted war and there was no open talk of independence. Congress respectfully petitioned the King for redress of grievances and called for a total boycott of trade with the Mother Country until things improved.

The Congress adjourned after six weeks and vowed to return in the spring if their grievances were not satisfied. The Second Continental Congress assembled in May 1775 to learn that things had changed radically. Blood had been shed at Lexington and Concord, and a passel of angry New England farmers had the British army in Boston under siege.

Hundreds of Philadelphia men formed militia units, and the city was filled with drilling recruits. Twenty-eight upper-class, fox-hunting buddies formed a cavalry unit, which became known as First City Troop.

The horsemen escorted George Washington whenever he came to Philadelphia and fought at the battles of Trenton and Princeton. The Troop is still galloping along as a National Guard unit. Its members are mostly from old Philadelphia families, and its armory museum proudly displays a tattered Hessian battle flag captured at Trenton.

Inside the State House, the Second Congress drafted an "Olive Branch Petition" declaring "devotion" and "affection" for the crown and begging his majesty to stop the war, repeal the laws against Boston and bring about "a happy and permanent reconciliation." But his majesty refused to read petitions from rebels.

War raged for a year before those cautious patriots in the State House decided it was time to declare independence and justify the rebellion with a proclamation to the world. Virginian Thomas Jefferson composed the document in rooms he rented in the house of bricklayer Jacob Graff, at the corner of 7th and Market. A replica of the Graff House now stands on the spot.

While the momentous decision on national independence was taking place, a new Pennsylvania constitution was pushed through, setting up the most radical, egalitarian political experiment of the era. It gave total power – with no checks by an executive or courts – to a one-house legislature, whose members were elected every year. Property qualifications for voting were abolished. Such freewheeling democracy frightened conservative patriots, who feared mob rule.

Meanwhile, the crucial vote came on July 2, 1776. Ten colonies were ready to vote for independence. But the delegations of Delaware and Pennsylvania were split, and New York was waiting for authorization from home.

Each colony had a different-sized delegation. Among the three Delaware delegates, one favored independence, one was opposed, and the third, Caesar Rodney, was absent. In a dramatic all-night, 80-mile gallop, Rodney arrived from Delaware at the last minute to break the tie and place Delaware on the side of independence.

Pennsylvania had a delegation of nine, but two were not in the city. Only Benjamin Franklin, lawyer James Wilson and farmer John Morton were committed to independence. Thomas Willing and Charles

Humphreys voted nay. John Dickinson and Robert Morris felt the time wasn't right for the break with England. Finally, Dickinson and Morris were persuaded to absent themselves from the final tally. Thus, Pennsylvania voted for independence by a slender 3-2 margin. New York abstained but joined the others a few weeks later.

After much politicking and maneuvering, the colonies had declared themselves "free and independent." John Adams was elated. He predicted that July 2 would become a great day of national celebration.

Jefferson's document was already written in anticipation of a favorable vote on independence. The Declaration of Independence was amended and passed on July 4. But the Declaration was not signed on July 4, and there were no celebrations or fireworks.

The document was given to Philadelphia printer John Dunlap, who dashed off 200 copies to be distributed across the new nation. One of the surviving copies was found hidden in the frame of a picture purchased in 1989 at a Lancaster, Pa., flea market for $4. It fetched $2.4 million at auction. An "engrossed" formal copy on parchment in the fine penmanship of Timothy Matlack, a rebellious Quaker expelled by the Friends, was signed on August 2.

It was July 8th when bells in Philadelphia rang all morning, announcing the first public reading of the Declaration in the State House yard. It is possible that the only bell that did NOT ring that day was the State House Bell, now known as the Liberty Bell. The steeple of the State House was badly rotted (it was torn down in 1781.) So, it might have been too dangerous to ring the bell.

The bell did not become a revered symbol of American independence until the 1840s, when abolitionists used its image in their literature and a now-forgotten writer, George Lippard, made the Bell an icon. In 1847 Lippard penned an imaginative magazine story in which an elderly bell ringer waits and waits in the State House steeple for word on independence. His young grandson has his ear to the door as the great men debate. At last, the youngster shouts up to the old man, "Ring, grandfather! Ring!" The story was reprinted endlessly, even published as truth by some 19th-century historians.

Independence Hall didn't take on the mantle of a sacred American shrine until the 1824 visit of the elderly Marquis de Lafayette. He was welcomed with great ceremony to the State House, and some began calling the Assembly Room the Hall of Independence. By then Pennsylvania government had moved to Harrisburg. The city purchased the building and leased the upper floor and Assembly Room to artist Charles Willson Peale for his natural history museum. The museum left the building in 1828.

By the middle of the 19th century, Independence Hall had been restored and a new steeple built. Despite the sentiment and affection now lavished on the building, city government established a dog pound in the basement in the 1850s.

WAR IN THE DELAWARE VALLEY

With the Congress directing the war from Philadelphia it was only logical that the British would try to capture the rebel capital and, perhaps, end the war.

In late 1776, American forces were driven out of New York and chased across New Jersey; it appeared that Philadelphia would fall and panic gripped the city. About half the population and the Continental Congress fled.

But Washington saved the day with his daring crossing of the Delaware on Christmas night, capturing nearly 1,000 Hessian mercenary troops in Trenton. He followed up Trenton with a second victory in Princeton.

Eighteenth-century armies did not fight in the winter, so Washington settled down in Morristown, N.J., while the British retired to New York and North Jersey. When warm weather returned, Gen. William Howe launched a new attack on Philadelphia, and this time he would succeed.

Here is a brief synopsis of battles in and around Philadelphia in 1777:

BRANDYWINE: Instead of marching through New Jersey, Howe loaded 15,000 troops aboard ships and sailed to the Chesapeake Bay, going ashore at Elkton, Md., about 50 miles south of the city.

Washington moved 11,000 men to the Brandywine Creek to block the oncoming British and Hessians. The two sides clashed on September 11. There was a good deal of skirmishing and artillery dueling around Chadd's Ford. Washington felt that all the shallow fords where troops could cross the Brandywine were covered. But local Tories led the British to an unguarded crossing, and the Americans found themselves outflanked. Washington managed to retreat in good order, but the way to Philadelphia was now opened to the enemy.

PAOLI: The British did not take the city immediately but followed Washington as he moved northwest to protect military supplies in and around Reading. Pennsylvanian "Mad" Anthony Wayne with some 1,500 men was ordered to stay close to the British rear and to harass the Red Coats with surprise attacks. But it was Wayne who was surprised.

On September 21, Wayne was camped only four miles from the British and planning an early morning attack. He did not believe the British knew his position, but they were well informed. The flints needed for firing their muskets were taken from the attackers. The Red Coats emerged from the woods at 1 a.m. and fell on Wayne's men silently with bayonets and swords. A British officer wrote that he could see the Americans by the light of their dying campfires. "Then followed a dreadful scene of havoc. The light dragoons came in, sword in hand. The shrieks, groans, imprecations, deprecations, the clashing of swords & bayonets etc. . . . was more expressive of horror than all the thunder of artillery."

Wayne managed to form up his men and make an orderly retreat. Perhaps 100 Americans were killed, including 53 buried on the battlefield. Many others were wounded. The Americans dubbed the defeat "the Paoli Massacre," employing it as anti-British propaganda. Wayne, a very competent and daring soldier, was court martialed at his own request and acquitted.

GERMANTOWN: The British marched unopposed into Philadelphia on the morning of September 26. Patriots fled. Tories cheered. Congress had already moved to Lancaster.

The majority of the British troops were camped about six miles from Philadelphia in the village of Germantown. Washington, a man of bold action, decided on a surprise attack. His complicated plan involved four separate columns converging from different directions in the center of the village at the same time. The plan was much too complex for amateur soldiers lacking modern communications, but there was initial success.

The morning of October 4 was exceedingly foggy, and all combatants were hampered by the heavy fog and smoke of battle. The major American thrust came straight down today's Germantown Avenue from Chestnut Hill. The first line of British defense – about 120 men led by Lt. Col. Thomas Musgrave – fell back and took shelter inside the large stone summerhouse, known as Cliveden, owned by Pennsylvania Chief Justice Benjamin Chew.

Rather than surround the house with a small number of men and advance to the center of Germantown as planned, Gen. Henry Knox ordered an all-out attack on Cliveden. Other units did advance. In the fog and confusion created by the battle going on behind them at Cliveden, Americans mistakenly fired on each other.

It had been a bloody morning for both sides. Despite initial success by the Americans, the British regrouped and held. More than 50 Americans died valiantly attacking the British soldiers barricaded inside Cliveden. Soldiers who had trudged 16 miles through the night and fought hard now had an exhausting return march to Whitemarsh.

While the attack on Germantown failed, the French were impressed with Washington's daring. Two weeks later, America scored its first major victory, with the surrender of an entire British army at Saratoga. The two actions convinced France to enter the war.

A beloved pet dog of Gen. Howe was lost during the confused fighting. A few days later, the dog, with its identifying name tag, was found by Continental soldiers. Washington returned the wayward pooch to his British counterpart along with a polite note.

FORT MIFFLIN/FORT MERCER: Philadelphia was in British hands but the Delaware River was not. No supplies or reinforcements could reach the British by water because the rebels had taken pains to create roadblocks. These included forts opposite each other on both riverbanks: Fort Mifflin or Mud Island just below the mouth of the Schuylkill, and Fort Mercer, also known as Red Bank, on the New Jersey side.

Spear-like obstructions known as cheveaux-de-frise (frizzy horse), designed to rip holes in a ship, were sunk just below the water's surface. An armada of small craft, known as the Pennsylvania Navy, added depth to the blockade.

Opening the river was crucial for the British, and Washington was determined to hold the forts. The Americans scored a stunning victory when German Col. Carl Emil von Donop led 2,000 Hessian troops in a land assault on Fort Mercer on October 22. The attackers were cut to ribbons; hundreds were killed, including von Donop.

That same night, two British warships ran aground near Fort Mifflin. One was the mighty 74-gun flagship, Augusta, which caught fire the next morning and blew up with such force that people in Philadelphia thought it was an earthquake. The second ship, Merlin, was set afire to keep it from falling into American hands.

But the British had Fort Mifflin surrounded by land and eventually managed to get their ships within firing range. In November those inside Fort Mifflin were subjected to six days of furious bombardment. The intensity of the bombardment was unprecedented, and its defense has been called "one of the most gallant actions of the war." When nothing was left to defend, Fort Mifflin was abandoned. The British found 50 unburied American corpses in the ruins. Across the river, Fort Mercer was abandoned as indefensible.

As a postscript, ingenious Yankee David Bushnell – who had invented a primitive one-man submarine known as the Turtle – hatched a scheme to blow up British ships in Philadelphia by floating kegs loaded with explosives down the river. One keg hauled out of the river exploded and killed a boy. The British lined the riverbanks, blasting away at the kegs and anything else that floated.

VALLEY FORGE: By late December the British had pulled their forces out of Germantown and set up a defensive ring around the city. Washington selected Valley Forge, 25 miles west of the city, for the American winter encampment.

The winter of 1777-78 was not particularly bitter or snowy, but there were terrible supply problems. Goods could not be delivered by water, roads were few and poor, the entire procurement system was inept and corrupt. There were severe shortages of food, blankets, clothing and shoes. About 2,000 of the 11,000 American troops arrived at Valley Forge shoeless. Illness was rampant; an estimated 3,000 died of disease during the winter. Horses died of starvation and exposure.

While the suffering was horrendous, the shortages eventually eased and a dramatic transformation took place in the Continental Army. By the end of the encampment, those ragged amateurs had become a professional, confident fighting force. The transformation was accomplished by a vigorous training regime directed by German volunteer Baron Friedrich von Steuben. For the first time, American soldiers mastered the tactics and skills necessary to move and maneuver in ranks and charge with bayonets. When the two sides next clashed in the open field at Monmouth, N.J., the Americans displayed a new military mastery and confidence. The battle was inconclusive, but it was the British who retreated this time.

William Penn was
22 years old and
not yet a Quaker
when this portrait
was painted of the
young aristocrat
wearing armor.

William Penn's second
wife, Hannah Callowhill,
was 24 years younger than
her husband. They had
seven children, but only
four lived to adulthood.

Benjamin West's famous and rather fanciful painting, "Penn's Treaty
with the Indians," was painted more than a century after the fact.

Benjamin Franklin was the 73-year-old American envoy to France when this marble bust was created by Jean-Antoine Houdon in 1779. It was recently acquired by the Philadelphia Museum of Art.

"Mad" Anthony Wayne was a daring and effective military leader whose one big mistake led to the so-called Paoli Massacre.

The Pennsylvania State House became known as Independence Hall after the 1824 visit of the Marquis de Lafayette. The classic Georgian structure was built between 1732 and 1748. The nation's most important documents, The Declaration of Independence and the United States Constitution, were debated and signed here.

Philip Syng Physick is rightfully called "The Father of American Surgery." He was the inventor of numerous surgical instruments and pioneered many surgical procedures. Among his patients were President Andrew Jackson and Chief Justice of the Supreme Court John Marshall.

Dr. Benjamin Rush was a fiery patriot and signer of the Declaration of Independence. He was among the city's outstanding physicians and has been called "The Father of American Psychiatry."

Pennsylvania Hospital, founded in 1751 with the aid of Benjamin Franklin, is the first and oldest hospital in America. The historic sections include an important art collection, the nation's oldest surgical operating theater and medical library.

Joseph Leidy was one of the world's great scientists of the middle 19th century. Trained as a physician, Leidy was a leader in many areas, including paleontology. He made the first accurate reconstruction of a dinosaur, discovered the cause of trichinosis and classified thousands of fossils.

Philadelphia's greatest Civil War hero was Maj. Gen. George G. Meade, the man who turned back Robert E. Lee's army at Gettysburg. Many of Meade's personal items and artifacts can be found in the city's two outstanding Civil War museums.

Proud workers at the Cramp shipyard in Kensington pose on the submarine Thrasher in 1910. For 113 years the firm built every type of vessel from wooden sailing ships to World War II fighting ships.

A group of visiting Native Americans from the West stops by America's most famous department store and meets with John Wanamaker. The well-known merchant accepts gifts of Indian paraphernalia from the visitors.

One of the city's outstanding 19th-century buildings is Founder's Hall at Girard College. Inspired by the Parthenon, it was designed by renowned architect Thomas U. Walter, who also designed the Senate and House wings and dome of the U.S. Capitol Building. The school for orphan boys is the legacy of childless merchant Stephen Girard.

One of the last remaining buildings of more than 200 structures created for the Centennial Exhibition in 1876 is Memorial Hall. It was created as a museum of art and was considered the fair's most handsome structure.

City Hall and the Philadelphia Museum of Art are connected by the Benjamin Franklin Parkway. The broad Parkway was inspired by the boulevards of Paris. More than 1,000 structures, mostly small houses, were demolished to create the Parkway. Logan Square, in the center of the Parkway, was made into a circle to accommodate auto traffic.

Philadelphia's past and present meld together throughout the city. Here colonial Man Full of Trouble Tavern, built in 1759, stands only yards from Society Hill Towers condominium complex, designed by architect I.M. Pei in the 1960s.

The massive Philadelphia Museum of Art and the 19th-century Water Works along the Schuylkill River are one of the city's most impressive views. The scenic Water Works was in operation from 1812 to 1911. Drinking water for the city was pumped to a reservoir where the Art Museum now stands.

A DIVIDED CITY, NATIONAL CAPITAL, YELLOW FEVER STRIKES

In June 1778 the British evacuated Philadelphia, deciding it was too difficult to hold and better to concentrate their strength in New York. The nine-month occupation set the stage for a period of instability, revenge and class conflict.

About 3,000 Tories left with the British. Included in the exodus was the Rev. Jacob Duche, rector of the joint congregations of Christ Church and St. Peter's Church. Duche loudly supported the American cause until the British came to town and then quickly switched sides. Another Tory refugee was wealthy Joseph Galloway, former speaker of the Pennsylvania Assembly and one-time friend of Ben Franklin. The Revolution split the city, dividing friends and families. The division was dramatically demonstrated when Benjamin Franklin's son, William, remained loyal to the crown.

Quakers found themselves in the eye of the storm. Their official pronouncements urged obedience to British authority and forbade support of the revolution in any manner. After the British evacuation, several Quakers stood trial for Tory activities. Two men hanged in Philadelphia for aiding the enemy were both Quakers. But even the Friends split. About 1,200 area Quakers were officially disowned for either taking up arms or supporting the Revolution in other ways. Some of the outcasts organized as "Free Quakers" or "Fighting Quakers" and built their own meeting house, which still stands at 5th and Arch streets.

After the suspected Tories were dealt with, division and hostility among the patriots surfaced along class lines. Working-class "leather aprons" resentment of Philadelphia's "silk stocking" elite stemmed mostly from severe inflation and shortages. Bitter workers hardly able to feed their families believed that merchants were profiteering. Silk-stocking gentry were critical of the excesses of the radical state government.

On Oct. 4, 1779, a mob of some 200 bitter militiamen, well lubricated with rum, decided to take out their frustrations on lawyer James Wilson, a signer of the Declaration of Independence who would become a major architect of the federal Constitution. Wilson identified with the merchant class. He was an outspoken critic of radical extremists and had defended Tories in court. Wilson and 20 of his friends – including two other signers of the Declaration – barricaded themselves inside his house at 3rd and Walnut. A gun battle followed that left five dead on the street and one fatality inside the house. First City Troop galloped to the scene and halted the bloodshed at what became known as "The Battle of Fort Wilson."

It wasn't the first violent clash; riots had occurred earlier in the year by sailors striking for higher wages. Even the city's military governor, war hero Gen. Benedict Arnold, was roughed up by a "mad, ignorant and deluded rabble." All the disorder would give Philadelphia a black eye when it came time to choose a national capital, but the chaos never approached a French Revolution. As prosperity returned, the old elite regained its prominence, and the radical state constitution was scrapped. Philadelphia settled into its traditional conservatism.

The new nation was really a loose confederation of 13 separate nations, each issuing its own money and pursuing its own foreign policy. In the sweltering summer of 1787, the State House was the venue for another gathering of the great national figures under the chairmanship of George Washington. The Constitutional Convention created a frame of government that has changed little over 200 years.

New York City was the temporary capital where, on April 30, 1789, George Washington was sworn in as the nation's first president. Among the first items of business was selecting a permanent capital. Philadelphians argued it should certainly be America's largest, most centrally located city. But there was the city's reputation for mob violence to contend with, and puritanical types felt Philadelphia was too world-ly, too wicked. Other Pennsylvania locations were floated, including a federal city in Bucks County opposite Trenton and a proposal on the Susquehanna River.

Philadelphia was the front-runner, but Virginia and New York were also vying for the capital. In the end, the matter was settled through political horse-trading. Among the hottest controversies was the desire by Washington and Treasury Secretary Alexander Hamilton to have the federal government assume $85 million in debt accumulated by the states. Generally, the North favored Hamilton's "assumption" plan, while was South was opposed. A deal was struck with Virginia. A new federal capital would be built on the Potomac River, and Virginia would support assumption. To appease Pennsylvania, the national capital would move to Philadelphia until Washington, D.C., was completed. The government and President Washington arrived in late 1790.

There was hope that once federal government settled into the Quaker City, it would decide to stay. Every effort was made at accom-modation. The house of financier Robert Morris at 6th and Market became the presidential mansion while Morris moved next door. It must have been a grand place because both British General Howe and Benedict Arnold had commandeered it as their residence. The Morris house was demolished in the 19th century, and a public restroom now stands on the spot where Washington once received visitors.

The city had completed two buildings flanking Independence Hall and turned both over to the new federal government. The courthouse became the meeting place for both houses of Congress, known as Congress Hall. Here three new states were added to the union and John Adams was sworn in as the second President. The City Hall became the meeting place of the U.S. Supreme Court, presided over by Chief Justice John Jay. Both buildings have been rehabilitated and are open to the public.

In a vain attempt to convince the federal government to remain, a grand Presidential Mansion was constructed at 9th and Market streets, but neither Washington nor Adams chose to live there. It was purchased by the University of Pennsylvania in 1800.

As the national capital, Philadelphia was an exciting place filled with foreign visitors and ambassadors. It was the scene of elegant parties, balls and receptions. The first natural history museum in America was established by portrait painter Charles Willson Peale. The largest theater in America opened at 6th and Chestnut, and the circus of equestrian John Bill Ricketts settled permanently in the capital.

A visitor from New England wrote of Philadelphia in 1790: "It is a large, populace, opulent and beautiful city, and ought undoubtedly be considered as the Metropolis of America."

But the glamour and excitement suddenly tumbled into dark tragedy as Philadelphia experienced the most catastrophic event in its history. In late summer of 1793 an epidemic of yellow fever broke out that became more deadly with each passing week. From late August into early November at least 5,000 people died out of total population of some 45,000. The city became a ghost town as those who could afford it fled to the country. Business ceased, and the only people seen on the streets were those hauling bodies and digging graves. Washington went to Mount Vernon. When he returned in November the disease hadn't yet abated, so he rented a house in Germantown.

There were heroes and villains during the crisis. Dr. Benjamin Rush and his assistants valiantly treated 100 or more people daily. Rush's treatment, however, was controversial. He insisted that the way to cure the disease was through massive bloodletting and massive doses of laxatives, which one critic called "a dose for a horse." Rush's regimen did cure a few but hastened the demise of many.

No one knew the deadly illness was caused by a virus transmitted by mosquitoes. The tropical disease was introduced by infected sailors and French refugees arriving in Philadelphia after the slave revolt in Haiti. Once a mosquito bit an infected person it would transmit the disease to others. Philadelphia had experienced yellow fever in the past and would be struck again (1,300 died in 1798), but nothing approached the tragedy and trauma of 1793.

CHAPTER 9

RIVER ICE, RIOTS AND INDUSTRY

The decades from 1800 to 1850 can be viewed in Charles Dickens' memorable words as the best of times and the worst of times.

Within a year Philadelphia lost its status as the capital of Pennsylvania and capital of the United States. In 1799 state government moved to Lancaster, then settled in Harrisburg in 1812. In 1800, the federal government moved to muddy, unfinished Washington, D.C.

Soon Philadelphia lost its first-place ranking as an American port, surpassed by New York and Baltimore. The city always had competitive disadvantages. New York is 200 miles closer to Liverpool. The long passage into the Delaware Bay and up the river is a treacherous gauntlet of shoals and shallows. Worse, the river froze. Each winter there were weeks, sometimes months, when no ships could move in or out of port. In January 1832, for example, 126 ships waited for the ice to break up. In 1837 the city took action by spending $70,000 for the first vessel built specifically as an icebreaker. Steampowered City Ice Boat #1 did yeoman's service until 1917.

The federal census of 1810 showed that New York had surpassed Philadelphia as the nation's largest city. Philadelphia would also lose its premier status in banking and finance to New York. Of course, Philadelphia's population did boom, spearheaded by a flood of poverty-stricken Irish Catholics.

The 1830s through the 1850s was a tumultuous, crime-ridden period for every American city. More than most, Philadelphia was wracked by lawlessness and bloody rioting. In some cases the Irish instigated the trouble; in other cases they were the victims.

But to suppose that the first five decades of the 19th century were marked only by decline and civil strife would be wrong. In many areas, Philadelphia was a model and trendsetter. It could claim honors as the nation's leader in science, architecture, civic improvements and physical beauty. The period also saw a crucial switch from shipping to industry that would make Philadelphia the nation's largest and most innovative center of manufacturing.

The city was undoubtedly a handsome place. The streets were neat, regular and tree lined. The profession of "architect" was new, and many of America's best architects lived and worked in Philadelphia. They created dozens of neoclassical gems, peppering the city with Greek and Roman temples, including William Strictland's Second Bank of the United States, based on the Parthenon. Thomas U. Walter's Founder's Hall at Girard College is an even more imposing Parthenon clone.

Philadelphia was incontestably the center of American science and medicine. It can be said that the Lewis and Clark Expedition began and ended with visits to Philadelphia. Here the expedition was equipped with the best gear, maps, medicines and scientific and surveying apparatus. Lewis took a six-week crash course with the nation's top scientific minds at the American Philosophical Society. (At the time, philosophy meant the whole of learning.) Most of the plant and animal specimens gathered were deposited in Philadelphia for study. The explorers' diaries were edited here by Nicholas Biddle. The explorers' portraits were painted by Charles Willson Peale.

The city was the nation's preeminent medical center, home of America's first medical school, first school of pharmacy and first professional organization for physicians. In Caspar Wistar the city had the nation's leading anatomist; Philip Syng Physick was the nation's foremost surgeon. Benjamin Rush is considered the "Father of American Psychiatry" for his work in treating the insane and authoring the first American book on mental illness. In 1825 Jefferson Medical College opened and soon challenged the University of Pennsylvania for honors as the city's largest and best medical school. In 1852 the first medical school for women in North America opened here.

Philadelphia was also the national center of book and magazine publishing. The Pennsylvania Academy of Fine Arts was America's first art school. The Peale Museum at Independence Hall was a fascinating attraction with its stuffed and live animals, portraits of the patriots and America's first reconstruction of an extinct animal, the bones of a mastodon.

Cultural, architectural and scientific achievements gave the city a certain luster and prestige. Just as important, Philadelphia got a head-start in the industrial revolution and would soon emerge as the nation's leading industrial city. From the start, William Penn recruited skilled artisans. In 1818 one writer commented, "There is no part of the world where in proportion to its population a greater number of ingenious mechanics may be found than in the City of Philadelphia."

Among those "ingenious mechanics" was John Fitch, builder in 1786 of the world's first steamboat. Another creative mechanic was Oliver Evans, inventor and pioneer builder of steam engines for a variety of chores. In 1804 Evans put together a steampowered, floating river dredge. He mounted the apparatus on a carriage and drove it down Market Street to the Schuylkill River, set it afloat and chugged to the Delaware. You might say that Evan's self-propelled, amphibious vehicle without rails was the first automobile.

Among these ingenious mechanics, Frederick Graff holds a place of honor. He was chief engineer and long-time superintendent of the city's remarkable Water Works on the Schuylkill River. The huge pumps were a mechanical wonder; the grounds surrounding the Works were an esthetic delight. The mechanical system was hidden below Greek and Roman revival buildings in a lushly landscaped setting that was Philadelphia's foremost beauty spot and a must-see tourist attraction. It has been said that Niagara Falls and the Philadelphia Water Works were the most popular landscape subjects for early 19th-century American artists.

Philadelphia's emerging industrial base was characterized by the large number and diversity of its shops and factories. The biggest industry was textiles, which would reign as king into the 1950s. During the first decades of the 19th century, thousands of weavers from Great Britain and Ireland worked at home on hand looms. There were still some 8,000 home-based hand weavers in the 1850s. But there were also 260 textile mills – more than any city in the world. By 1900 there would be some 700 textile and related firms, employing 60,000. Philadelphia mills turned out rugs, hosiery, woolen and cotton goods. Quality Germantown linen and woolens became famous.

There were reasons other than ingenious mechanics to explain why Philadelphia became so industrialized so early. A major factor was the huge deposits of hard anthracite coal in northeastern Pennsylvania and the discovery of how to burn it to generate steam-power. By the 1820s, canals, and later railroads, were delivering tons of hard coal to Philadelphia. About 40 local shops sprang up to manufacture the boilers needed to power all those mills and factories. By 1838 more steam engines were generating power in Pennsylvania than any other state.

Another development promoting industrialization was the founding in 1824 of the Franklin Institute for the Promotion of the Mechanic Arts. Today the Franklin Institute is the city's premier science museum. In the 19th century it was a dynamic organization that educated artisans and mechanics in practical science, mathematics and drafting. It was a "think tank," testing and developing inventions and technological advances. Its founders and faculty were among the city's brainiest scientists and innovators. It published a technical journal and sponsored competitions for inventors. The Institute won worldwide attention with an intensive research project on water wheels – the world's first scientific investigation of hydraulic principles to determine the most effective and efficient way to harness waterpower.

But the birth of the Industrial Age exacted a huge price in social upheaval and turmoil. The population exploded. In each decade from 1800 to 1850 the population of the city and surrounding communities increased by around 30 percent. Most of the newcomers were rural-born, unskilled, uneducated immigrants living in overcrowded, narrow "trinity houses" in back alleys and courtyards. There were no minimum wage, unemployment benefits or governmental "safety net" for the poor.

It was an explosive situation, marked by unrest, lawlessness and ethnic and class friction. It is difficult today to grasp the deep hatred and suspicion dividing Catholics and Protestants or to understand the malice exhibited by poor and working class whites towards blacks.

It is also difficult to imagine such a seething city without a police force. But there were no police or effective law enforcement. Instead, there were elected constables, night watchmen and a county sheriff who could do little to control the turbulence aside from seeking the help of citizen volunteers or requesting the militia. Even if the city had effective police, it would not solve the entire problem. Much of the lawlessness occurred in communities just outside the city's narrow boundaries, in crowded Kensington, Northern Liberties, Southwark, Moyamensing, Spring Garden and Schuylkill.

More than 50 violent street gangs ruled patches of the urban turf. The more notorious gangs included the Killers, Schuylkill Rangers, Skinners, Deathfetchers, Blood Tubs, Hyenas, Smashers, Rats, Bouncers and Gumballs.

Dozens of volunteer fire companies in and around the city served as social clubs and hangouts for macho young men. Many evolved into fighting gangs that battled each other on the streets and at fire scenes. Sometimes they set fires and waited to ambush rival companies. The fire companies adopted distinctive tattoos, and firehouse gangs served as political enforcers and election-day goons.

Starting in the mid-1830s violence against individual blacks and all-out race rioting involving hundreds became commonplace. (See Chapter 15.)

Sometimes the violence stemmed from the low industrial wages of the day. The hand-loom weavers often struck and demonstrated when contractors cut their rate of compensation. Strikers attacked and destroyed the equipment of weavers who refused to join the work stop-page. Striking weavers once pummeled the county sheriff. Mobs even attacked citizen posses.

Public drunkenness, brawling and assaults were commonplace, especially among the Irish Catholics. One cannot underestimate the festering hatred that the Protestant working class felt toward the "papists." Many truly believed that these impoverished immigrants were part of a papal conspiracy. One day, on a signal from the Vatican, they would rise up. Led by "wily Jesuits," they would violently take over America.

In the late 1830s an anti-Catholic "native American" political party formed in Philadelphia, calling itself the American Republicans. The strength of its paranoid platform was demonstrated in 1844 in the bloodiest riots of the century.

Four days of fire and blood were triggered, in large part by a rumor that a Catholic member of the school board interfered with daily Bible readings at one school. Readings from the King James Bible and study of the text were mandatory. But Catholics recognized only their own Douay version. Catholic Bishop Francis P. Kendrick had quietly negotiated a compromise allowing Catholic students to leave class during Bible readings and to use the Douay version for study.

The agreement sparked misunderstanding and provided the nativists with a hot-button issue. In a move guaranteed to ignite conflict, the American Republicans held a rally on May 7, 1844, in the heart of an Irish area at 3rd and Jefferson in Kensington. The Protestants were met with bricks, stones and gunfire. A 19-year-old Protestant apprentice, George Shiffler, was killed. The native Americans now had a "holy war" complete with a martyr. They returned, well armed. When the combat ended, two Catholic churches and a convent had burned to the ground; the mob cheered as the steeples collapsed. Dozens of Irish dwellings were torched, scores were injured, at least six killed. The sheriff was unable to control the mob, and a reluctant militia arrived too late.

The level of violence and the disgrace of church burnings dismayed city leaders, who were determined to use the full force of the militia if more rioting occurred. Round Two was not long in coming. The confrontation came in July at St. Philip Neri Catholic Church in Southwark, where a protestant mob took offense at arms stockpiled inside the church to defend against possible attack. After a series of misunderstandings and unwise decisions by militia leaders, a pitched battle took place on the streets around the church, pitting a mob of 2,000 against militia and mounted cavalry. The rioters even rolled out cannons, sparking an artillery duel. The cavalry galloped into the fight. The mob was defeated and the church saved, but two militiamen were killed and at least 12 rioters were slain. For several weeks 5,000 militiamen, from across the state, patrolled city streets.

The bloodshed and lawlessness shocked the city. Everyone could see the desperate need for police. On the other hand, both outbreaks of rioting had occurred just outside of city limits. There could be no law and order unless the surrounding boroughs, townships and districts were brought under a single jurisdiction and patrolled by one police force.

In addition to all the social unrest there was a particularly poignant tragedy during this period. A late-night fire in the city orphanage broke out on Jan. 24, 1822, with 90 children sleeping inside and the doors locked for security. Twenty-three orphans perished in the flames.

CHAPTER 10

A CONSOLIDATED CITY AND CIVIL WAR

The bloody anti-Catholic riots of 1844 would have at least two consequences: Philadelphia would develop the strongest Catholic school system in the nation and there would be a new, large police force patrolling a sprawling new city.

The riots precipitated a momentous event in city history: On February 2, 1854, Gov. William Bigler signed a law consolidating 29 municipalities and districts of Philadelphia County into one king-size city.

With the stroke of a pen, Philadelphia's population grew from about 125,000 to more than 500,000. In area, the city ballooned from two to 129 square miles. Population was concentrated along the Delaware River and stretched westward for a mile or two. Beyond these crowded areas were 1,500 farms, wetlands and woods.

The consolidation was motivated by the overwhelming need to police the unruly, fragmented urban sprawl. It would also improve water, streets, transportation and other services for all. Of course, some would lose power, so pushing through the change took a decade of political maneuvering. Now townships and villages, including Germantown, Frankford, Manayunk, Moyamensing, Roxborough, Kingsessing and Byberry, were merged into one municipality.

One characteristic of Philadelphia today is the large number of distinct neighborhoods and strong neighborhood identification. This parochialism is rooted in a time when most neighborhoods were, indeed, separate villages. It would take 100 years before all those farms inside city limits disappeared under asphalt and brick. As late as 1940 there were 239 small farms within the city. It wasn't until the 1960s that the last few farms in Eastwick and the Northeast disappeared.

There was also a move to disband the plethora of often warring volunteer fire companies and hire professionals, but the tradition was too strong, and that change would wait until the 1870s.

The mayor headed the new 900-man police department. The first mayor under consolidation, Robert Conrad, was elected with the support of the American nativists, and he hired only American-born cops. The next mayor, Richard Vaux, expanded the force to 1,000 and did hire Irish police. Vaux was a patrician who enjoyed joining the policemen on their nightly rounds and leading them in two-fisted attacks on the city's street gangs. The police broke the power of the gangs by behaving like a gang. Unfortunately, policemen were political appointees, beholden to the parties and party bosses. The politicians' iron hold over the hiring and firing of cops would haunt the city into the next century.

Philadelphia was far from peaceful after consolidation. It was bitterly divided over the question of slavery. Paradoxically, the city was a hotbed of abolitionist activity while the masses tended to be deeply racist, resentful and often violently hostile to antislavery activists. The Quakers and the city's large black population were deeply immersed in agitation and Underground Railroad activity. But most Philadelphians considered these militants dangerous radicals engaged in illegal, treasonous activity.

Most white Philadelphians, for instance, were as alarmed and angry about John Brown's attempted slave insurrection as the average Southerner. On the day Brown was hanged, local abolitionists held a memorial meeting that also attracted a hostile mob. Only a massive police presence prevented violence. A mass meeting led by business leaders adopted a resolution "to assure our brethren from the South that there exists a determined spirit to assert and maintain the Constitution of the Union and the rights of States under it." When Brown's body arrived by train in Philadelphia on its journey to New York state for burial, a mob gathered at the train station. Police used a decoy coffin to lure away the angry crowd while the real body was hustled away.

Philadelphia's geography – the state just north of the Mason-Dixon Line – along with close political, cultural and economic connections explain its pro-Southern tilt. The South was Philadelphia's best customer for luxury goods. The city's textile factories were tied to southern cotton. In addition to business ties, there were numerous family connections. A prime example is Pierce Butler, a Philadelphian who inherited his grandfather's (the Pierce Butler who signed the U.S. Constitution) vast plantations and 500 slaves in Georgia. Many southerners owned homes in Philadelphia or sent sons to the city for education. Of 630 students at Jefferson Medical College on the eve of the Civil War, 419 were southerners. The percentages were similar among the 360 medical students at the University of Pennsylvania. About 400 southern medical students left the city en masse on the eve of war.

Philadelphia went for Lincoln in the election of 1860, but business leaders adopted a resolution declaring that Pennsylvania should hold a convention to consider that it "might be released from its own bonds from the Union." Lawyer and civic leader Benjamin Harris Brewster declared it was uncertain whether Pennsylvania would go with the North or the South "or stand by herself."

As war approached, Philadelphia merchants were busy filling orders and shipping massive amounts of goods south. In the first months of the war, federal authorities constantly confiscated merchandise, including rifles, scheduled for delivery to the Confederacy.

Once blood was shed, the city's masses rallied to the Union, while the majority of the upper-class aristocracy remained pro-South and anti-war. Those members of the elite with strong Union leanings founded a separate club to express their patriotism, the Union League. The local Union League broadened its base and grew to 1,000 members by the close of the war. The League became a bastion of the Republican Party and remains one of the city's largest and most prestigious private clubs.

Fort Sumpter, S.C., fell on April 14, 1861, without a fight. The first casualties of the Civil War came four days later when four Massachusetts soldiers and five from Philadelphia were killed by pro-Southern rioters in Baltimore. The unarmed troops were being rushed by rail to Washington and had to change trains in Baltimore, where they were attacked by the mob.

Philadelphia was an important military medical center during the war. The government built two huge hospital complexes: the Satterlee Hospital in West Philadelphia with more than 3,000 beds, and the sprawling Mower Hospital in Chestnut Hill with 4,000 beds. There were smaller government hospitals and a score of private hospitals treating the Union sick and wounded. The state chartered a hospital ship and special railroad cars to bring wounded men to the city. Rail cars arrived from Washington several times each week packed with injured men.

As in every war since, Philadelphia played a key industrial role. The Navy Yard, then at the foot of Federal Street, was busy churning out vessels, and so were several private shipyards. The government's Frankford Arsenal, founded in 1816, had 1,200 employees working round-the-clock to produce ammunition. Textile mills were operating at full steam making military blankets and uniforms.

The war made some rich. Butcher Peter A. B. Widener became wealthy supplying meat to the Union Army. He would later control the city's many streetcar companies and branch into other businesses. Widener was worth about $25 million when he died in 1903. Banker Jay Cooke sold a billion dollars in war bonds for the government and became one of America's richest men. Mill owners John and James Dobson amassed a fortune manufacturing army blankets in East Falls.

Philadelphia was shaken when General Robert E. Lee's army invaded Pennsylvania. Hundreds of volunteers and laborers started digging fortifications around the city. The scare passed, and the South's military fortunes declined after Lee's defeat at Gettysburg. The man who turned back Lee's army was Maj. Gen. George G. Meade, Philadelphia's greatest war hero. Thousand of artifacts from the conflict are preserved in former Civil War veterans posts in Center City and Frankford that are now outstanding Civil War museums.

CHAPTER 11

INDUSTRIAL MIGHT AND A MIGHTY FAIR

Philadelphia, with a good head-start, would rightfully claim title as the nation's leading industrial center in the years following the Civil War. And when America celebrated its 100th birthday in 1876, the city would throw a mammoth party highlighting the new machine age.

Unlike Pittsburgh, Detroit or New England's mill towns, Philadelphia would never be dependent on just one industry. There were 7,000 manufacturers by the end of the 19th century, making every product imaginable. Flourishing industries produced toys, cigars and tobacco products, beer, candy, paper boxes, fine leather, drugs, rope and twine, paint, umbrellas, nuts and bolts, hats, printing, sugar and oil refining.

Oddball firms included the S.S. White Dental Works, whose 300 to 500 workers made millions of false teeth, dental instruments and dental supplies. Eighteen firms were making steel files in 1885; the Black Diamond File Works boasted of producing "750 files and rasps per day." Eleven firms manufactured steel springs. Ninety marble companies employed 1,900 workers. A.J. Reach & Co., founded in the 1880s, produced baseballs and baseball gloves, employing 1,000 workers by the early decades of the 20th century.

Small and medium-sized manufacturers were the rule, but there were a few giants. Baldwin Locomotive Works was the city's largest single employer, with 17,000 workers at its peak. English immigrant Matthias W. Baldwin created the first American-made locomotive in 1832 and grew into the world's largest locomotive builder. The sprawling Baldwin plant at Broad and Spring Garden streets sold steam engines to railroads around the world, turning out three times the number of locomotives as its nearest competitor. Another firm claiming "world's largest" status was Henry Disston's Keystone Saw Works. Started by one man in 1840, it grew to a 64-acre riverfront complex in Tacony with 2,500 workers, most living in a company town. The largest maker of saws of every size and type was famous enough to merit a two-hour visit by President Rutherford B. Hayes in 1879.

At the close of the Civil War an obscure New Jersey-born hatter, John B. Stetson, came to Philadelphia and found scores of competitors. Young Stetson succeeded with a fresh idea. He perfected a broad-brimmed hat for the western market, and his firm grew to become the world's largest hat-maker. By 1915, the paternalistic Stetson firm had 5,400 workers in a 25-building factory complex in North Philadelphia.

The city's many foundries were making and exporting all sorts of machine tools. William Cramp and Sons shipyard on the Delaware was building fighting ships for America's Great White Fleet, Russia, Japan and Turkey.

Of course, no American city came close to Philadelphia's dominance in textiles. By the turn of the century there were some 700 textile and related firms, employing a quarter of the city's work force.

Call it the "Industrial Age,"or the "Machine Age," the world was changing at a rapid pace, and Philadelphia was the American city leading the exciting transformation.

A grandiose idea took hold after the Civil War to celebrate the nation's 100th birthday with a huge international fair. America had never before seen anything like the mammoth Centennial Exhibition on the west side of Fairmount Park. It dealt little with patriotism and history; its major themes were science, technology, machinery, commerce, inventions, and human progress.

The Exhibition cost $10 million. Although it was closed on Sundays, it attracted 10 million visitors, almost a quarter of the nation's population. More than 200 buildings were erected. The Main Building, covering 21 acres, was the world's largest building. Fifty foreign nations exhibited. Each of six restaurants could feed 5,000 at one time. The world's widest bridge was built over the Schuylkill River at Girard

Avenue to carry traffic and pedestrians to the fairgrounds. A new railroad depot was built outside the fair. There was even a railroad to take visitors around the grounds. Landscaping included lakes, scores of statues, monuments, fountains and 20,000 shrubs and trees.

On opening day, May 10, 1876, a crowd estimated at 200,000 listened to a 1,000-voice choir sing the Centennial Hymn by John Greenleaf Whittier. Among the 4,000 dignitaries on hand were President Ulysses S. Grant, both houses of Congress, the U.S. Supreme Court and the Emperor of Brazil. Grant led the dignitaries to Machinery Hall, where the President and Emperor Dom Pedro of Brazil pulled levers starting the world's largest steam engine, created by George H. Corliss of Rhode Island. The Corliss Engine was one of the marvels and icons of the Centennial. The 680-ton giant stood five stories high and developed up to 2,500 horsepower. It powered all the machinery in the exhibition.

Among the marvels that wowed the crowds was a mechanical calculator with 15,000 precision parts that could compute logarithms and other mathematical calculations. Alexander Graham Bell astounded visitors with his telephone. A youthful Thomas Edison introduced a telegraph that could transmit four messages over one line. The typewriter was seen for the first time.

The exhibition included tons of arts and crafts, household goods and horticultural and agricultural buildings, but it was American ingenuity and efficiency in technology that had worldwide influence. The event changed America's image abroad. A British engineer who visited the fair wrote, "We are losing our former leadership, and it is passing to America."

German scholar Franz Reuleaux wrote a series of newspaper articles on the Centennial entitled "Letters from Philadelphia," which became an influential book. Reuleaux excoriated German goods as "cheap and bad" and lauded American machinery as "practical," "clever," "the best in the world." In 1941 Adolf Hitler expounded on the transformation of German industrial production from "cheap and bad" to "superior." The Fuhrer dated the dramatic turnaround to "the world's fair in Philadelphia."

The Centennial Exhibition was also a high-water mark for Philadelphia self-pride and self-esteem. Most out-of-town press coverage was positive. A Chicago newspaper declared Philadelphia was "as cosmopolitan as Paris."

Philadelphia would try to duplicate the success of the Centennial fair again in 1926 with a 150th-anniversary Sesqui-Centennial Exposition, which generated only moderate excitement and few out-of-town tourists. The city would dream of doing something big and spectacular for the nation's bicentennial in 1976. For all the talk, it would produce nothing more than scattered, uninspiring cultural and entertainment events.

CIVIC PRIDE
AND POLITICAL CORRUPTION

From the 1870s through the 1920s Philadelphia would create great public buildings, grand boulevards and beautiful parks. New colleges and cultural institutions would rise. There would be massive construction of housing, reaching 4,500 brick row houses a year and the creation of extensive transportation systems.

Paradoxically, all the expansion, improvements and farsighted thinking happened under politicians and a political machine that were infamous for corruption. In his 1903 muckraking classic, *"Shame of the Cities,"* Lincoln Steffens begins his evaluation of Philadelphia with these words: "Other American cities, no matter how bad their condition may be, all point with scorn to Philadelphia as worse; `the worst-governed city in the country.'"

Steffens titled this chapter: "Philadelphia: Corrupt and Contented." More than a clever phrase, "corrupt and contented" is a nugget of truth. There were periodic reform efforts, but Philadelphians displayed an amazing indifference to the shenanigans and graft of a notorious GOP machine.

One explanation for this complacency was that politicians could point to real achievements. A prime example was the new, grandiose City Hall, which took 30 years to complete (1871-1901) and cost $20 million — more than double the original estimate. Kickbacks and graft partially explain the extravagant price tag, but the building is truly monumental. Its 548-foot-high tower, supported by 22-foot-thick granite foundation walls, is the tallest structure without a steel frame in the world. With more than 14 acres of floor space and some 600 rooms, it was for some time the world's most spacious building. It is arguably America's most decorated public building, festooned with scores of statues, ornamental stonework all capped by the 37-foot-high statue of William Penn.

Other grand buildings sprouted around City Hall. In 1882 the Pennsylvania Railroad built the castle-like Broad Street Station attached to the world's largest train shed. By the mid 1890s hundreds of trains carrying 60,000 passengers were coming and going every day.

On the east side of City Hall, merchant John Wanamaker had taken over an abandoned railroad depot, hired 600 salespeople and drawn huge crowds of customers during the Centennial celebration. The pious Wanamaker was a department-store pioneer and a retailing genius. Among Wanamaker "firsts" are the white sale, telephone ordering and electric lighting. In 1911, Wanamaker tore down the depot and built the present store (now Lord & Taylor), with President Wiliam Howard Taft on hand for the dedication.

Just before the Centennial, Philadelphia opened America's first zoological gardens in Fairmount Park. The park – 4,000 beautifully landscaped acres along the Schuylkill River and Wissahickon Creek – was born in the 1850s out of the need to protect the city's water supply from contamination. Some 400 properties along the two streams, including colonial mansions, mills and factories, were purchased at a cost of $6 million. Most structures were demolished. By the 1880s, Philadelphia had a park that was one of world's largest, prettiest and well used.

And by the 1880s, the city's Republican Party ruled supreme. In 1881 the city elected its last Democratic mayor until 1952. And Democrat Samuel King managed to squeeze out a narrow victory only with the support of a GOP reform organization.

An example of how the GOP political machine delivered benefits to the city and profits to the corrupt is the Roosevelt Boulevard, a wide roadway that opened the undeveloped Northeast section of the city. Beginning in 1902, a syndicate composed of top politicians purchased the land at low cost and then sold it to the city for the unneeded road at enormous profits. The city was paying $2,500 an acre for land purchased just a few years before for $300. The highway was rerouted by a mile and a half overnight to profit one politician and punish another. The $1.4 million boulevard-construction contract went to politician-contractor "Sunny" Jim McNichol.

Today one looks at the 12-lane (Theodore) Roosevelt Boulevard – the longest, widest, busiest street in the city – and marvels at the farsightedness of those 1902 planners. In fact, it was a boondoggle labeled by critics at the time, "The McNichol Boodlevard."

Another McNichol-GOP boondoggle that saved countless lives was a water-filtration plant. Before its completion in 1907, more than 1,000 Philadelphians a year were dying of typhoid fever traceable to the city's polluted water. It was the highest typhoid death rate of any American city; three times that of New York. Nearly $25 million was paid to McNichol and a few small contractors to build the Torresdale Filtration Plant between 1899 and 1907. In 1905 a political feud sparked the mayor to have honest engineers examine the project. The engineers reported that contractors and city officials pocketed $6 million of the $16 million spent to date, even allowing McNichol a 20 percent profit.

The other major "contractor bosses" of the era were brothers, George, Edwin and William Vare. They were born on a South Philadelphia pig farm and became trash haulers and political powers. The brothers set up a number of companies and won hundreds of city contracts for street cleaning, trash hauling, road building and repair, bridge and sewer construction. The Vares received at least 341 contracts totaling $28 million over a 30 year period.

During the decades of machine rule there was no such thing as a fair election in Philadelphia. "The machine controls the whole process of voting and practices fraud at every stage," Steffens wrote. He cites a district with fewer than 100 legal voters who cast 252 votes. When a registered letter was sent to every voter in another locale, 63 percent came back undelivered. Six houses in another division had 172 voters. Because every police officer owed his job to the politicians, police were part of the election machinery used to harass foes and protect those perpetrating fraud.

Violence was often part of election strategy. The most egregious example came in a 1917 primary battle between GOP factions for a City Council seat in the "Bloody 5th Ward," better known today as Society Hill. The Vare faction hired 18 gunmen from the Bronx for strong-arm duties on Election Day. Precinct police were informed that they were not to interfere with the out-of-town goons. The gangsters — armed with guns and blackjacks — raided the headquarters of the rival faction and attacked the anti-Vare city council candidate on the street. A plain-clothes detective, unaware that the goons were operating under police protection, rushed to the candidate's aid and was shot dead. Even in Philadelphia this was beyond the pale of dirty politics.

The gunmen, several policemen and politicians, including Mayor Thomas B. Smith, were charged in connection with the homicide. For once, the blasé citizens of Philadelphia were enraged. A mass meeting demanded reform, but soon the normal levels of corruption and contentment were restored.

In addition to the "rake-off" from contracts, the machine was oiled by salary kickbacks of one to four percent paid by every city employee, including cops and teachers.

The city GOP machine was controlled from the top by the state party boss. The system had been pioneered by U.S. Sen. Matthew Quay of Beaver County, a canny "kingmaker" in national politics. His protégé and successor as senator and state party boss was Philadelphia aristocrat Boies Penrose. Quay, and later Penrose, had the power to choose the mayor of Philadelphia, the governor of Pennsylvania and influence the selection of the Republican candidate for president.

Penrose was a Harvard graduate who loved to play the game of politics. He was an infamous glutton capable of downing a dozen eggs, a one-pound ham steak and quarts of coffee for breakfast or polishing off an entire turkey for dinner.

When Penrose died in 1921, distinguished Philadelphia lawyer George Wharton Pepper was appointed to fill his Senate seat. But in the next election William Vare decided he wanted to be senator. Vare spent lavishly to win a three-way GOP primary and then beat Democratic rival William B. Wilson for the seat.

Both primary and general elections reeked of shameless fraud.

Wilson petitioned the Senate to investigate the vote. Vare was denied his seat while a committee spent three years probing the matter. Among other irregularities, the committee found 25,000 false entries in Philadelphia voter-registration books. Ballot-box stuffing was widespread; thousands of dead people and children had voted. The committee concluded that only one in eight votes cast in Philadelphia was legitimate. For the first time, the Senate voted not to seat a member.

Although the GOP machine seemed to control most everything in Philadelphia – including Democratic leaders on the Republican payroll – it did not control the press. Periodic newspaper exposés and calls for reform had little lasting effect. The bosses were too entrenched, too efficient. Little could be accomplished without the machine. It was an organization that could deliver the goods and the jobs on a local, state and national level.

WAR, BOOTLEGGERS, DEPRESSION

It's not surprising that Philadelphia was a major producer of military goods during World War I, but two war-related events are worth noting: The seemingly overnight rise of America's (perhaps the world's) largest shipyard and a ghastly influenza epidemic that killed at least 15,000 Philadelphians.

The government-financed Hog Island Shipyard with 50 shipways rose along the Delaware River, where the Philadelphia International Airport now stands. It took only 11 months from groundbreaking until the first ship was launched. The war ended three months later. But Hog Island's 30,000 workers completed 122 cargo and transport ships before the vast operation shut down in 1921.

Those Philadelphians alive in the fall of 1918 would always harbor vivid and horrifying memories of the great Spanish flu pandemic. Worldwide, the outbreak took an estimated 30 million lives. Some historians say no American city suffered as much as Philadelphia. At its height, 700 Philadelphians died every day.

As with yellow fever in 1793, the city virtually came to a halt. People shunned each other, public events were canceled and the great challenge was burying the dead. There were not enough hospital beds, caskets or grave diggers. Bodies piled up in the morgue. Fortunately, the epidemic abated after six weeks.

In 1919, the state legislature, with the backing of boss Boies Penrose, gave Philadelphia a new-reform city charter. One major change was scrapping the ancient two-house city legislature (Common Council and Select Council) for a single 21-member City Council. There were a dozen other positive changes that seemed – on paper – to guarantee real reform in City Hall. However, the ever-resourceful, Vare-led Republican machine found ways around every reform measure, and nothing changed. Even the Civil Service Commission was staffed by party hacks.

With the advent of prohibition of alcoholic beverages, city government and law enforcement sank to new depths of corruption. Bootlegging and the illegal sale of liquor were a bottomless well of graft. In 1928 one magazine declared the city was home to 1,185 open bars, 13,000 speakeasies and 300 brothels, paying an estimated $20 million in bribes to police and politicians. One bank was said to have $10 million in bootleggers' deposits.

The average citizen was drinking more than ever and scornful of the law. However, the public was alarmed by a frightening rise in gangsterism. A thriving criminal underworld perpetrated endless bank robberies, payroll heists, burglaries, hijackings, extortion and murder. In 1924, newly elected Mayor William F. Kendrick promised to appoint an honest, nonpolitical public safety director to head the police department. The mayor did a better job than he intended. Kendrick appointed Marine hero Brig. Gen. Smedley Darlington Butler, who took leave from the service to work in Philadelphia. Twice awarded the Congressional Medal of Honor, Butler saw action in the Spanish-American War, the Philippines, the Boxer Rebellion, World War I and several interventions in Latin America.

The honest leatherneck launched an energetic crackdown on demon rum, raiding sleazy dives and big Center City hotels. None of the politicians, including the mayor, was pleased by Butler's zealous performance, though the crackdown went for naught. Corrupt magistrates invariably let the culprits off. During Butler's one-year reign more than 10,000 speakeasy owners and bootleggers were arrested. But fewer than 500 actually paid a fine. The Marines refused to extend Butler's leave, so he resigned. But Mayor Kendrick had had enough and fired the much-too-honest Marine.

The 1920s saw completion of the city's most ambitious beautification project: wide, leafy Benjamin Franklin Parkway leading to an imposing new Art Museum looming on the hill William Penn called Fair Mount. The idea of a grand boulevard connecting Fairmount Park and Center City was first proposed in 1871, inspired by the impressive boulevards then opening in Paris.

But it wasn't until 1907 that the project got underway. More than 1,000 properties, including two hospitals, were eventually purchased and demolished. Total costs approached $30 million, which included the normal amount of graft. Several outstanding planners and architects participated in the Parkway's design, including two Frenchmen.

Construction on the Art Museum began in 1919, and the massive Greek temple opened in 1928. The panoramic view of the city skyline from the top of the museum's 72 steps never fails to impress. Several wealthy art collectors were involved in the project, and the vast building's 200 galleries filled quickly with impressive works of art.

The 1920s also saw a construction boom in high-rise office buildings in Center City. Honoring tradition, none rose above City Hall. The first bridge connecting central Philadelphia with New Jersey opened in 1926. The 1.8-mile, $37 million Delaware River Bridge (renamed the Benjamin Franklin Bridge in 1955) briefly held a world record for longest suspension bridge. Cars were banned on opening day while a crowd, estimated at 250,000, walked to Camden.

The Sesqui-Centennial Exposition of 1926, celebrating the nation's 150th anniversary, was underfunded, behind schedule and plagued by constant rain. Its one lasting structure was massive Municipal Stadium at the southern end of Broad Street. The most memorable event of the fair was the first Jack Dempsey-Gene Tunney heavyweight championship fight, which drew 120,757 to the new stadium, setting a crowd record at a sporting event. The stadium was a white elephant, rarely used except for Army-Navy football games between 1936 and 1980. Few mourned when it was demolished in 1992.

Philadelphia weathered the Great Depression of the 1930s better than many other cities because of the diversity of its industry. At its worst, the city's unemployment rate ran about 12 percent for native-born whites and about 20 percent for blacks and the foreign born. Yet the national average hit 25 percent. Some cities, including Toledo, East St. Louis and Akron, hit a jobless rate of 50 to 60 percent.

Still, for thousands of Philadelphians life was a desperate struggle. By June 1932 all relief funds – city, private and state – were exhausted, and aid to 52,000 families was suspended. The poorest turned to church and union soup kitchens for survival. The state stepped in two months later with a relief program providing food, clothing and heating fuel.

Hard times saw the comatose Democratic Party come to life, but still unable to elect a mayor until 1952. New leaders replaced Democratic hacks supported by the GOP machine. The machine doled out some patronage jobs to the "rival" party and paid rent for Democratic headquarters. Whether Democrat or Republican, Philadelphia contractors got involved in politics. The new Democrats were led by contractors John B. Kelly (an Olympic rowing champion) and Matthew B. McCloskey, along with real-estate mogul Albert M. Greenfield. In 1932 Franklin D. Roosevelt almost won the city, and in later elections, FDR scored overwhelming victories. But the entrenched GOP successfully held City Hall.

World War II ended the depression. Industry sprang to life, and Philadelphia couldn't find enough workers. In the early stages of the war, the Frankford Arsenal produced just about every round of American military ammunition. Cramp's shipyard, which closed after the First World War, was in full operation again. Some 30,000 were working round-the-clock at the U.S. Naval Shipyard. About the same number of workers were turning out fighting ships across the river in Camden at the private New York Shipbuilding Co.

Baldwin Locomotive, now located in suburban Eddystone, was producing tanks. The Disston Saw Company made armor plate and so did Midvale Steel. In all, about 3,500 Philadelphia businesses were making defense supplies. Philadelphians had cash in their pockets again but nothing to spend it on.

The city saw the deadliest accident in its history on Sept. 6, 1943, when a fast-moving Washington-to-New York passenger train derailed in Frankford. Seventy-nine passengers were killed and 120 were injured. Doctors were amputating legs on the spot to free trapped victims.

CHANGE AT CITY HALL, INDUSTRY VANISHES, TOURISM TOUTED

World War II was over, and the 67-year rule of the Republican Party machine was about to end.

The city's population in the 1950 census stood at an all-time high at just over two million. Industry seemed as strong as ever. Newer firms were churning out modern goods: televisions at Philco, Plexiglas at Rohm and Haas, instrumentation at Honeywell.

Slum clearance and urban-renewal projects were on the drawing boards. In 1950, the wisest prophet could not predict that Philadelphia's glory days were numbered. But within a decade the trends were clear: population was declining, industry was vanishing, urban renewal had failed. Large sections of "the city of homes" were characterized by abandoned homes and a hopeless underclass.

Even the change at City Hall meant a continuation of one-party rule. The corrupt and complacent GOP was simply replaced by an all-powerful Democratic organization that would produce its own scandals and scoundrels.

The decline of manufacturing, a middle-class stampede to the suburbs and urban decay were syndromes plaguing all old Eastern and Midwestern cities. While hard hit, neither hope nor civic pride ever died in Philadelphia. There were success stories. The city stubbornly maintained many of its unique traditions and institutions.

The reform movement and Democratic Party hegemony were spearheaded by two Social Register patricians: Joseph S. Clark and Richardson

Dilworth. They operated as a team. Dilworth ran unsuccessfully for mayor in 1948 with Clark as his campaign manager. But the GOP's grip on the city was slipping. The following year, Dilworth was elected city treasurer while Clark won the controller's office. By agreement, it was Clark's turn to run for mayor in 1952, and he won by 124,000 votes. Dilworth was elected district attorney, and Democrats swept City Council. Soon the city's Republican Party faded into near extinction. Clark went on to the U.S. Senate. Dilworth would win two terms as mayor and then resign to make an unsuccessful run for governor.

Voters approved a new city charter in 1951, streamlining government and placing more power in the mayor's office. Clark and Dilworth brought in professional managers and planners, but in many cases their decisions — based on expertise — were worse than those, made by the old political shysters, based on greed. Federally subsidized housing projects for the poor were a miserable failure.

What was hailed as the nation's largest urban-renewal project, on 2,500 acres of land in southwest Philadelphia known as Eastwick, displaced 5,000 households. A viable neighborhood was destroyed and replaced by insipid row houses and garden apartments with no sense of community.

Another urban-renewal project in Northern Liberties destroyed an enclave of poor blacks and Eastern European immigrants, but little was built to replace the demolished houses. Developers promised an upscale "city within the city" called Franklintown just north of Center City. Old houses and factories were cleared, but the grand plans failed to materialize.

The reformers' most notable success was revitalizing the decaying 18th- and 19th-century houses of Society Hill into one of the most charming and desirable residential neighborhoods on the East Coast.

Population loss could have been much worse, but the city had vast undeveloped stretches in the Northeast. Thousands of families that might have fled the city were able to purchase modest new houses in the decades after World War II. In 1940 there were only 1,800 units of housing between Pennypack Creek and the city's border with Bucks County; the number soared to 58,783 by 1990. Population in the same district rose from 26,736 to 163,371 during the 30 years from 1950 to 1980. But the Northeast was an exception to the decades of population decline that followed the 1950 census high-water mark.

In many cases people followed jobs. In the 1950s, the textile and apparel firms began moving South or simply folding. Scores of obsolete 19th- and early 20th-century factories closed. Among the industrial giants that died were Disston, Philco, Curtis Publishing, Fels Soap, Midvale Steel, Jack Frost Sugar, Cramp's shipyard, Baldwin locomotive, Stetson hats and J.C. Brill, once a leading maker of buses and trolleys. The federal government closed its 110-acre, 246-building Frankford Arsenal complex in 1977. The shadow of closure hung over the Naval Yard for decades. Finally, after 194 years, the end of the Naval Yard came in 1995 with the loss of 7,000 jobs.

Among the most shocking failures was the Philadelphia-based Pennsylvania Railroad, which celebrated its 100th birthday in 1946 and proudly proclaimed itself "the world's largest railroad" with 156,182 employees. By the 1960s the railroad kingpin was ill and combined with rival New York Central in the largest American business merger of its times. The largest merger was followed in 1970 by the nation's largest bankruptcy.

Another shocking death in the family of Philadelphia institutions was the demise in 1982 of the Philadelphia Bulletin just months before its 135th anniversary. It had once been North America's largest evening newspaper, with a daily circulation of 770,000.

Racial friction had been a fact of life in Philadelphia since the early 1800s. In 1964 black anger was mounting across the nation. In Philadelphia, two days of rioting and looting raged in the North Philadelphia ghetto, sparked by a minor traffic arrest and wild rumors. When it ended, 600 businesses were destroyed or damaged, 600 people were arrested and 340 were injured, including 100 policeman. A lively nine-block business district along Columbia Avenue (now Cecil B. Moore Avenue) was destroyed and never recovered.

In 1962, Philadelphia got its first Catholic mayor, James H. J. Tate. Tate elevated colorful and controversial policeman Frank Rizzo to the post of police commissioner. The ambitious Rizzo, promising a crackdown on crime, followed Tate as mayor in 1972, serving two terms. In 1984 the city got its first African-American mayor, W. Wilson Goode. Its first Jewish mayor, Edward Rendell, was elected in 1992.

Rizzo, who inspired either adulation or bitter enmity among Philadelphians, set the wheels in motion for the worst financial crisis in Philadelphia history by agreeing to overgenerous labor contracts with city employees. Goode, a bureaucrat with few political skills, did nothing to avert financial collapse. Rendell took office with a budget deficit of $250 million, stacks of unpaid bills, and the lowest bond rating of the nation's 50 largest cities.

Rendell won national attention and acclaim by setting the city's finances in order and actually producing small budget surpluses. His ebullient personality and aggressive salesmanship inspired optimism for the city's future. The loss of population and jobs slowed in the 1990s, but both trends continued. There were about 25,000 abandoned buildings and 15,000 vacant lots in the city in the mid 1990s, and those numbers rose as the decade ended.

As the 20th century closed, Philadelphia's population was somewhat less than 1.5 million. In 50 years it had lost a quarter of its residents. Only sad vestiges of the city's industrial might remain. Philadelphia's largest private employers are universities, hospitals and utilities.

There were times during the last quarter of the 20th century when the city seemed cursed by an unending series of bizarre crimes and singular tragedies.

During a 1975 state convention of the American Legion at the venerable Bellevue Stratford Hotel, a mysterious and deadly respiratory illness struck. Twenty-nine legionnaires died and 151 were stricken with an illness that was eventually traced to a virus breeding in the hotel's air-conditioning system.

A radical cult called MOVE and its deadly confrontations with police in 1978 and 1985 brought the city worldwide notoriety. The first clash with the armed group at its Powelton Village house in 1978 ended in the death of a policeman. Another policeman and several firefighters were wounded. Nine cult members were sentenced to long prison terms.

On May 13, 1985, police attempted to dislodge MOVE members from a house they fortified in Southwest Philadelphia. Despite 9,000 bullets fired into the house, a stalemate ensued that ended in a spectacular fire. A satchel bomb dropped by police from a helicopter on MOVE's rooftop bunker set off an inferno that killed 11 inside the house, including five children, and destroyed 62 houses.

Deadly Mafia warfare raged through the 1980s. The nation was horrified by murderous Gary Heidnik, convicted of enslaving, torturing, dismembering and cooking the flesh of two women in his North Philadelphia house in 1987. Three other victims found chained in the basement survived. He was executed in 1999.

In another bizarre case, Dr. Martin Spector, an ear, nose and throat specialist, was arrested after leaking packages containing five human heads were found by a parcel service. For 20 years Spector had been buying body parts from morgue attendants and selling them to researchers.

In 1993 came the tale of Edward "Uncle Eddie" Savitz, a quiet accountant with an odd sexual fetish. For decades Savitz had been paying teenagers for their dirty underwear, socks and feces. As the century neared its end, 70-year-old Marie Noe confessed to suffocating eight of her infant children between 1949 and 1967.

Never-ending scandals in the police department ranged from the corrupt "few bad apples" to systematic underreporting and misreporting of crimes to create a false impression of low crime rates.

On the positive side, the city enters the 21st century with a handsome, new $500-million convention center, sparking a surge in hotel construction and conversions of old buildings to hotels. Tourism, entertainment and festivals to attract visitors and suburbanites to the city were touted as keys to the future. Indeed, Philadelphia is blessed with a plethora of museums, historic sites, good restaurants, theaters and other attractions. Unlike many cities, the central business district is healthy, lively at night and surrounded by attractive residential neighborhoods.

One of the city's most appealing attributes is its reverence for tradition and the amazing continuity of so many of its institutions. About 250 years ago, Benjamin Franklin helped found America's first hospital, lending library, fire insurance company and learned society. Still going strong are Franklin's Pennsylvania Hospital, the Philadelphia Library Company, the Philadelphia

Contributionship for the Insurance of Houses from Loss by Fire and the American Philosophical Society.

The Civil War put an end to slavery, but the Pennsylvania Abolition Society still meets. The oldest social club in the nation, The State in Schuylkill, clings to traditions that are nearly 270 years old. The New Year's Day tradition of costumed, strutting Mummers has roots in the city's colonial past. First City Troop, founded in 1775, still stands ready to saddle-up for battle.

It's an interesting city with its own distinctive flavor and feel. Let others consume tacos and Twinkies. Philadelphians salivate over greasy cheesesteak sandwiches, foot-long hoagies. They like scrapple for breakfast, soft pretzels with mustard for a snack and a bowl of snapper turtle soup laced with sherry wine to start dinner.

Philadelphia's appeal lies in its variety of architecture; its distinct neighborhoods; a large, lush park system; extensive public art; its enduring and unique traditions. An important component of its allure lies in its long, rich history and the surprising preservation of so much of its past.

THE SAGA OF BLACK PHILADELPHIA

Those who want an understanding of the mindset, attitudes and situation of African-Americans today can obtain real insight by studying 300 years of black history in Philadelphia.

There was a handful of blacks in the Delaware Valley when Penn arrived. Today they make up nearly half the city's population. Being a loving, tolerant Quaker didn't stop Penn from owning slaves. His will provided for their freedom, but he was in debt at the time of his death and the slaves were sold.

Likewise, being a sagacious Renaissance Man didn't prevent Benjamin Franklin from owning household slaves for 30 years. While his wife, Deborah, was a tenderhearted mistress, Franklin seemed oblivious to the injustice of slavery until he became the American spokesman in England. There he was forced to confront the hypocrisy of slave ownership by those screaming so loudly about rights and liberty. In old age, Franklin became an eloquent foe of slavery and president of the Pennsylvania Abolition Society.

There is one recorded shipload of 150 slaves arriving for sale in Philadelphia. Mostly they came in small "parcels" of a few individuals along with goods from the Caribbean.

No more than 1,500 slaves ever resided in the city. The average slaveholder had only a few individuals; most often they lived in the same house as their white masters. They were servants or worked in shops at various trades and crafts by the side of their masters.

It was said to be a "mild" form of slavery compared to the Southern plantation system. Yet, Philadelphia's slaves ran away frequently, committed suicide at a high rate, and had a death rate 50 percent higher than whites and an abnormally low fertility rate.

In 1688, German Quakers in Germantown issued the first American protest condemning slavery. But major Quaker merchants continued to traffic in slaves, and individual Friends continued to own blacks. Conscience-stricken Friends, however, never let the issue rest. In 1758, Quakers condemned members involved in the slave trade. But it wasn't until 1776 that Friends were told to free their slaves or face expulsion from the faith.

The Revolution pricked the conscience of many, and in 1780 Pennsylvania passed the nation's first abolition law – although not a single slave was freed. The law banned slave trading in the state. Any child born to slave parents after passage of the law (March 1, 1780) would be freed at age 28. This gave the slave owner time to recoup the costs of caring for a small child too young to work.

Only 400 slaves and about 800 free blacks lived in Philadelphia when the law passed. As the 18th century drew to a close, Philadelphia became a magnet for newly freed slaves from nearby places and runaways from the South. The city's black population tripled during the 1790s; by 1820 there were 12,000 blacks in the city, nearly 11 percent of the population.

One reason for the influx – in addition to the availability of work – was the support of liberals and abolitionists in Philadelphia combined with the start of black self-help organizations, black schools and churches. Some established small businesses, and a black leadership emerged. A few, such as sailmaker James Forten (1766-1842), became wealthy or well-known such as Francis Johnson, band leader and song writer.

But as their numbers grew so did white animosity and fears. In 1805, a mob chased blacks who gathered at Independence Hall for July 4th festivities. The next year, bills in the Pennsylvania legislature to bar blacks from migrating to the state were introduced but failed. A visitor to the city in 1809 noticed young white boys insulting blacks on the streets, with their parents approval. There were emerging patterns of housing segregation. The northern city with the largest black population was becoming the North's most bigoted city.

In 1818 a major brouhaha emerged when blacks began raising funds to create a volunteer fire company. The city's 40 fire companies were vehemently opposed, declaring it was impossible to work in close cooperation with blacks. The furor was so intense that Forten and other leaders convinced the aspiring firemen it would be best to scrap their plans.

Irish immigrants began to push blacks out of traditionally low-paying jobs such as stevedores and coachmen and attacking them physically. Blacks were lampooned in vicious cartoon caricatures in local newspapers. Members of the black elite were physically attacked when entering a fancy ball, for the sin of dressing fashionably. A three-day race riot in August 1834 saw blacks attacked, killed and beaten both on the streets and inside their houses.

Piles of abolitionist pamphlets were ceremonially tossed into the Delaware River by bigots. When the abolitionists found it impossible to rent meeting space, they built their own large auditorium, Pennsylvania Hall, near 6th and Race streets. As soon as it opened in May 1838, a crowd of several thousand surrounded the place and burned it to the ground. For good measure, the mob burned a black orphanage and attacked a black church.

Bigotry became government policy in 1838 when the state legislature disenfranchised Pennsylvania's black voters. Blacks did not regain the vote until passage of the 15th Amendment in 1870. When jubilant blacks lined up at the polls in 1871, whites attacked in the southern part of the city. Four were murdered, including Octavius Catto, the city's foremost young black leader.

By the 1860s the city was crisscrossed by horse-drawn trolley lines, but blacks couldn't ride. Gaining admission to the trolleys became the first organized civil-rights struggle in Philadelphia. Blacks brought suit in court. They were arrested for attempting to enter the forbidden cars. A state judge dismissed one suit brought by the black community, declaring, "It is too much to expect a race long civilized to travel with those just emerging from the shades of barbarism." The mayor said he would "not wish female members of his family to sit with Negroes."

One newspaper editorialized that contact between the races would lead to sexual attacks on white women. One company polled its riders on the question; passengers were overwhelmingly opposed to the integration of streetcars.

Finally, in 1867 legislators from other parts of the state passed a law banning discrimination on the cars. "Philadelphia stands disgraced before the world. . . . It is the last city that inflicts this cruel barbarity upon a redeemed race," declared Sen. Morrow B. Lowry of Erie.

It wasn't until 1944 that the first black streetcar motormen and conductors were hired under orders from the federal Fair Employment Commission. This sparked a wildcat strike of 2,000 white transit workers, paralyzing the city and preventing countless defense workers from reaching their jobs. President Franklin D. Roosevelt ended the walkout by sending troops to the city.

As Philadelphia grew into one of the world's most industrialized cities, its black citizens sank lower into poverty, despair and resentment. The factories were hungry for labor, but blacks were frozen out of industrial jobs. While countless immigrants from every part of Europe were absorbed into the factories and mills, bosses refused to put blacks on the assembly lines. They argued that white workers would refuse to work side-by-side with blacks. The result, they said, would be walkouts and violence.

One researcher says only one percent of Philadelphia's black working population found employment in the new factories. Instead, 76 percent were classified as unskilled laborers or domestic and service workers. Only 28 percent of new immigrants held these low-level jobs. The one exception to the rule was the Midvale Steel Company in the Nicetown section, which hired black workers and allowed blacks to rise to foremen without experiencing a white backlash.

Skilled factory workers in the 1890s could make $20 a week. Pick-and-shovel laborers earned half that amount. In his 1899 study, W.E.B. DuBois declared that 90 percent of Philadelphia's African-American families fell below the poverty line. Blacks often played the role of strikebreakers at the turn of the century, a role that bolstered white hatred, but netted few permanent jobs.

Blind bigotry and ignorance did not die with slavery. At the end of the 19th century, a doctor at Hahnemann Hospital declared that some blacks (like rattlesnakes) "have small poison sacks or cells under their gums which in certain circumstances eject poison."

During the industrial revolution, crime rates dropped for whites and rose for blacks. Police and politicians tolerated vice in black areas but mostly suppressed it in white neighborhoods. Thus, black neighborhoods were "zoned" for vice and crime.

Many blacks looked to education as the answer to discrimination. DuBois saw clearly that "education will get you nothing but disappointment and humiliation." Philadelphia businesses, banks and shops refused to hire blacks for clerical, sales and other white-collar jobs. The city's black base was too poor to support even a handful of black lawyers in this period. All had to supplement their incomes by selling insurance or real estate. City government employed a few token blacks in menial jobs such as messenger.

Black police were first hired in 1881 by a courageous Mayor Samuel King. But when black officer James N. Reaves was hired in 1940, African-American cops walked (they never rode) beats only in black neighborhoods. The highest-ranking black policeman was a sergeant. On the rare occasions that Reaves arrested a white suspect, he first called for white officers to assist. Reaves rose to become Philadelphia's first black police captain in the mid-1950s and daringly integrated patrol-car crews for the first time.

It took World War II before blacks were hired in any numbers in Philadelphia's factories and mills. Now there was opportunity. By 1960, 28 percent of the black working force had factory jobs while the white percentage dropped to 21. Just as blacks settled into secure industrial work, America was entering a postindustrial age.

Thousands of blacks had moved north, but Philadelphia's huge textile industry was moving south. Some factories followed the white stampede into the suburban ring. During the 1950s and 1960s most of North Philadelphia, West Philadelphia, Germantown and sections of South Philadelphia seemed to go from white to black almost overnight. With the loss of industry, once-vibrant working-class black neighborhoods became forlorn ghettos strewn with vacant houses, empty lots and dead business streets.

Even the old Philadelphia practice of lampooning blacks died hard. Part of the Mummers Parade tradition involved strutting white "dudes" and "wenches" in blackface makeup. The threat of violence finally ended Mummers' blackface in 1964.

Blacks had minimal political clout even in the 1950s and 1960s, as they emerged as the city's largest ethnic/racial group. Those blacks elected to local office seemed to match the level of their white counterparts: mostly party hacks, incompetents, rascals and scoundrels. Finally, in 1984 Philadelphia elected its first black mayor, W. Wilson Goode, and to the astonishment of many, re-elected Goode in 1988. Goode, an unimaginative bureaucrat, left office with city finances in shambles and a mood of despair for Philadelphia's future.

THUMBNAIL PROFILES OF OTHER NOTABLE PHILADELPHIANS

RICHARD ALLEN (1760-1831): Remarkable ex-slave (he purchased his own freedom). Powerful preacher. Founded African Methodist Episcopal (AME) denomination. Organized black volunteers for yellow fever epidemic of 1793 and black militia unit during War of 1812.

NICHOLAS BIDDLE (1786-1844): Handsome, erudite, blue blood. Edited the diaries of Lewis and Clark. President of the Second Bank of the United States. Lost "bank war" with President Andrew Jackson. His Andulusia estate on the Delaware River, Bucks County, still stands.

JOHN CADWALADER (1742-1786): Wealthy merchant. Member of prolific ex-Quaker family. Headed militia unit of Philadelphia elite. Participated in battles of Princeton, Brandywine, Germantown and Monmouth. Declined offers of high rank in Continental Army but retained leadership role in militia. Fought duel with Thomas Conway to defend Washington's honor.

ALEXANDER MILNE CALDER: Scottish-born sculptor. Created the myriad of statues and decorative elements on City Hall, including the 27-ton statue of William Penn. Son, Alexander Sterling Calder, created Swann Fountain on Logan Square. Grandson, Alexander (no middle name) Calder, creator of art mobile. Calder mobiles at Art Museum and local Federal Reserve Bank.

RUSSELL CONWELL (1843-1925): Civil War veteran who got religion. Baptist preacher. Founder of Temple University, three hospitals, 3,000-seat Temple Baptist Church. Raised money by giving the same

"Acres of Diamonds" speech 6,000 times.

CYRUS H.K. CURTIS (1850-1933): Poor boy from Maine. Rose to great wealth and influence by creating middlebrow magazines, Ladies Home Journal and Saturday Evening Post. Uncanny ability to pick good editors and build circulation. The Curtis School of Music founded by daughter.

GEORGE MIFFLIN DALLAS (1792-1864): Son of treasury secretary, Alexander J. Dallas. Mayor of Philadelphia. U.S. Attorney. U.S. Senator. Ambassador to Russia. Vice President under James Polk. Dallas, Texas, is named in his honor.

STEPHEN DECATUR (1779-1820) Fearless, swashbuckling naval hero of wars against Barbary pirates and War of 1812. Died in duel with Commodore James Barron. Buried at St. Peter's Episcopal Church.

LYDIA DARRAH or DARRAGH (dates unknown): Simple Quaker housewife who overheard British plan for attack on Washington's army at Whitemarsh in December 1777. Passed through British lines to give timely warning. Story once thought a legend is now accepted as fact.

ANTHONY J. DREXEL (1826-1893): Son of founder of Drexel banking firm. (J.P. Morgan partner in New York branch.) Shrewd businessman, noted philanthropist. Promoted industrial and technical education for working class students by establishing the Drexel Institute of Technology.

EDWIN FORREST (1806-1872): America's great tragic actor. Mercurial and combative, his rivalry with British actor William C. Macready led to May 10, 1849, riot in New York City, which killed 30. The titillating details of his divorce from beautiful actress Catherine Sinclair provided a newspaper field day. Home at Broad and Master streets is now Freedom Theater.

REBECCA GRATZ: (1781-1869): Renowned for beauty, intelligence and philanthropy. One of 10 children of German-Jewish merchant Michael Gratz. Believed to be the model for character Rebecca in Sir Walter Scott's novel *Ivanhoe*. Never married. Religion prevented marriage to true love, Presbyterian Samuel Ewing.

STEPHEN GIRARD (1750-1831): French sea captain stranded in Philadelphia at outbreak of American Revolution. Became city's most important merchant. America's richest man. Key financier of War of 1812. His wealth created Girard College for orphan boys.

SAMUEL GROSS (1805-1884) Pennsylvania Dutchman; learned English at 15. Premier physician/surgeon/medical educator. Prolific medical writer. His book on military surgery used by both sides in Civil War. Thomas Eakins' painting of Gross in surgery at Jefferson Medical School considered an American masterpiece.

OTTO HAAS (1873-1960) German-born founder with Dr. Otto Rohm of Rohm and Haas chemical firm. Rohm invented Orophon to soften animal hides, eliminating use of animal dung. Haas started branch in Philadelphia in 1909 because city was center of kid leather industry. His wealth funds the charitable William Penn Foundation.

ABSALOM JONES (1747-1818): Very literate slave. Worked endless hours to raise money to free his wife, purchase a house and, finally, his own freedom. Established St. Thomas African Episcopal Church (1794). First black ordained as Episcopal priest.

FRANCES ANN "FANNY" KEMBELL (1809-1893): Beautiful English actress. Married and divorced Philadelphia-based Georgia plantation owner Pierce Butler. Published scathing attack on slavery, also a journal with impressions of America and life in Philadelphia.

ELISHA KENT KANE (1820-1857): Physician. Adventure traveler. Arctic explorer. Wrote best-selling books on two failed attempts to find the lost John Franklin expedition in Canadian Arctic. Buried at Laurel Hill Cemetery.

JOSEPH LEIDY (1823-1891): Perhaps, America's top scientist of the mid-19th century. The ultimate generalist: physician, anatomist, paleontologist, biologist, parasitologist, naturalist, microscope expert. Discovered the cause of trichinosis. Classified fossils. First accurate reconstruction of a dinosaur. Transplanted cancer cells to frog. Beloved Penn professor.

JAMES LOGAN (1674-1751) William Penn's secretary ran colony with great skill. Scholar. Master of many languages. Owned largest library in early America. Plant expert. Became rich in fur trade and real estate. His Germantown country manor, Stenton (1730) open to public.

ROBERT MORRIS (1734-1806) High-rolling, high-living merchant-banker. Signer of Declaration of Independence. Raised cash for the Revolution but made profit, too. Turned down Washington's request to be first treasury secretary. Graciously lent his house at 6th and Market for use as Washington's presidential mansion. Unfortunate land speculation wiped out wealth. Spent three years in debtors' prison.

S. (SILAS) WEIR MITCHELL (1829-1914): Leading American neurologist and popular novelist. Expert on snake venom, nerve damage and mental breakdown. Introduced "the rest cure" for neurosis. Patients came from all over world. Novels included best-seller *Hugh Wynne, Free Quaker.*

LUCRETIA MOTT (1793-1880): Quaker. Leading national abolitionist. Founder of Female Anti-Slavery Society. Helped launch female civil-rights movement at 1848 Seneca Falls, N.Y., convention.

ROBERT PURVIS (1810-1898): Unflagging antislavery activist, Underground Railroad leader and champion of black civil rights. Child of wealthy white southerner and mixed-race mother. Refused to "pass" as white.

ELIZABETH GRISCOM "BETSY" ROSS (1752-1836): Quaker-born seamstress. Married three times. First two husbands died during Revolution. Circumstantial evidence and legend credit her with sewing first American flag.

JOSEPH WHARTON (1826-1919): Descendant of early settlers. Pioneer in making zinc for galvanizing iron and smelting nickel. Founder of firm that became Bethlehem Steel. Acquired 150-square-mile Wharton Tract in Pine Barrens of New Jersey. His belief that college should prepare students for the real world of business led to founding of University of Pennsylvania's prestigious Wharton School of Finance.

RECOMMENDED READING

Bacon, Margaret H. *The Quiet Rebels. The Story of the Quakers in America.* New York. Basic Books Inc. 1969.

Burt, Nathaniel. *The Perennial Philadelphians: The Anatomy of an American Aristocracy.* Boston. Little Brown. 1963.

Chidsey, Donald Barr. *Valley Forge.* New York. Crown Publishers. 1959.

Dorwart, Jeffery M. *Fort Mifflin of Philadelphia.* Philadelphia. University of Pennsylvania Press. 1998.

Eberlein, Harold D. and Hubbard, Cortlandt. *Diary of Independence Hall.* Philadelphia. J.B. Lippincott. 1948.

Gifford, Edward S. *The American Revolution in the Delaware Valley.* Philadelphia. The Pennsylvania Sons of the Revolution. 1976.

Kelley, Joseph J. *Life and Times in Colonial Philadelphia.* Harrisburg. Stackpole Books. 1973.

Lane, Roger. *William Dorsey's Philadelphia & Ours.* New York. Oxford University Press. 1991.

Langguth, A. J. Patriots. *The Men Who Started the American Revolution.* New York. Simon and Shuster. 1987.

Lewis, Arthur H. *The Worlds of Chippy Patterson.* New York. Harcourt, Brace and Company. 1960.

Maass, John. *The Glorious Enterprise: The Centennial Exhibition of 1876 and H.J. Schwarzmann, Architect-in-Chief.* Watkins Glen, N. Y. American Life Foundation. 1973.

McCaffery, Peter. *When Bosses Ruled Philadelphia. The Emergence of the Republican Machine, 1867-1933.* University Park. Pennsylvania State University Press. 1993.

Nash, Gary. *Forging Freedom: The Formation of Philadelphia's Black Community, 1720-1840.* Cambridge. Harvard University Press. 1988.

Powell. J.H. *Bring Out Your Dead: The Great Plague of Yellow Fever in Philadelphia in 1793.* Philadelphia. The Unversity of Pennsylvana Press. 1949. Reprinted 1993.

Reaves, James N. *Black Cops.* Philadelphia. Quantum Leap Publishers. 1991.

Stutz, Bruce. *Natural Lives. Modern Times. People and Places of the Delaware River.* New York. Crown Publishers. 1992.

Tussell, John B.B. *William Penn: Architect of a Nation.* Harrisburg. Pennsylvania Historical and Museum Commission. 1980.

Various editors. *William Penn and the Founding of Pennsylvania 1680-84.* Philadelphia. University of Pennsylvania Press. 1983.

Weigley, Russell F., editor. *Philadelphia: A 300-year History.* New York. W.W. Norton & Co. 1982.

Weslager C.A. *New Sweden on the Delaware: 1638-1655.* Wilmington. Middle Atlantic Press. 1988.

INDEX

NOTES